Akadjé Richard Alloukou

Analysis of the health decentralization policy in Côte d'Ivoire

Akadjé Richard Alloukou

Analysis of the health decentralization policy in Côte d'Ivoire

Operationalization of deconcentration and devolution in health

ScienciaScripts

Imprint
Any brand names and product names mentioned in this book are subject to trademark, brand or patent protection and are trademarks or registered trademarks of their respective holders. The use of brand names, product names, common names, trade names, product descriptions etc. even without a particular marking in this work is in no way to be construed to mean that such names may be regarded as unrestricted in respect of trademark and brand protection legislation and could thus be used by anyone.

Cover image: www.ingimage.com

This book is a translation from the original published under ISBN 978-620-2-27345-9.

Publisher:
Sciencia Scripts
is a trademark of
Dodo Books Indian Ocean Ltd. and OmniScriptum S.R.L publishing group

120 High Road, East Finchley, London, N2 9ED, United Kingdom
Str. Armeneasca 28/1, office 1, Chisinau MD-2012, Republic of Moldova, Europe
Printed at: see last page
ISBN: 978-620-5-78799-1

TABLES OF CONTENTS

DEDICATED 2
ACKNOWLEDGEMENTS 3
SUMMARY 4
LIST OF ABBREVIATIONS AND ACRONYMS 6
1 Introduction 8
2 Rationale for the study 10
3 Objectives 12
4 Review of the literature 13
5 Methodology 21
6 Results and analysis 24
7 Proposed Strategies 40
8 Limits 49
9 Recommendations 50
10 Conclusion 53
Bibliography 54
Annexes 59

DEDICATED

I dedicate this book

To the Lord God Almighty, maker of heaven and earth, to him belongs all the glory (Psalms 27).

To my father who left me during the ITM training, may his soul rest in peace

To my wife Mireille, my children Pura, Keren and Rebecca, my Mother Therese and all my Family for all their love and untiring support in word, gesture and thought which made my studies a success.

ACKNOWLEDGEMENTS

To the Belgian government, in particular to the Belgian Development Cooperation (DGD) which offered me this opportunity through the scholarship

To all the ITM staff and in particular to the teachers, supervisors and social and academic support teams who gave us the benefit of their immense knowledge and accompanied us throughout our stay at ITM and throughout Belgium

To my memory guide, for his availability and the quality of the exchanges, which were very enriching

To Professor Samba Mamadou, Director of Prospective, Planning, Evaluation and Health Information (DPPEIS) and all the staff for their support

To Dr. Bassalia Diawara, Director of Health Training and Research (DFRS) for introducing me to decentralization issues

To Dr. Tahet Noël, Deputy Director General of Decentralization and Local Development (DGDDL) for all administrative documentation

To Dr. Nahounou Noël, Country Director of Abt Associates/HFG/USAID for his support

To all the colleagues of the MPH class of 2016-2017

May God Almighty return it to you beyond your expectations.

SUMMARY

Introduction

Decentralization is a process that has been taking place in Côte d'Ivoire since independence. It has accelerated, particularly in the form of deconcentration and devolution, since the economic crisis of the 1980s and under pressure from donors. It is based on arguments of efficiency, rationality, responsiveness of services to the needs of the population, permanent contact between citizens and local authorities, and its capacity to increase community participation (1-3).

Since the year 2000, decentralization in its devolution form has been deepened by the creation of several types of Territorial Communities and the transfer and distribution of competences from the State to the Territorial Communities or local governments.

However, ownership and implementation of these competencies are lacking, resulting in fragmented planning and coordination of local health activities, weak accountability mechanisms and quality of care, and inefficient health action.

General objective

Contribute to the operationalization of deconcentration and devolution by strengthening the planning and coordination system of health activities at the local level.

Methodology

This study used a case study approach that allowed for secondary data collection by reviewing the literature on decentralization in low- and middle-income countries. We used documents from the Ministry of Health and the Ministry in charge of Territorial Administration as well as our own experience.

A conceptual framework combining Bossert's "decision space" approach (4) and Brinkerhoff's "community empowerment" approach (3) was used to analyze the data. Results were triangulated with the literature from low- and middle-income countries to ensure data quality.

Results and analysis

After a review of the literature and documentation on decentralization in low- and middle-income countries, we carried out an in-depth analysis of the decentralization and devolution pair using a framework adapted from Brinkerhoff (3), combining the decision space developed by Bossert (4) and community empowerment. The work then focused on the case studied, which is the coupling of deconcentration and devolution through the regional planning process for health development, in the context of Côte d'Ivoire. The study reveals that the two administrations, the deconcentrated services of the Ministry of Health and the local governments, have difficulties in collaborating for various reasons, including

- the top-down, non-incremental and non-participatory implementation of the decentralization process (deconcentration and devolution) and the transfer of competencies from the State to local governments;

- the incompleteness and inadequacy of the legislative, regulatory and institutional framework for decentralization;
- Weak capacity of local actors and governance and accountability mechanisms;
- Fragmentation of planning and coordination of health activities at the local level.

In view of these problems, we have proposed four strategic axes to resolve them in order to improve the implementation of deconcentration and devolution in the health sector in Côte d'Ivoire. These are:

- strengthening the legislative, regulatory and institutional framework;
- capacity building of local actors;
- strengthening governance and accountability;
- Improving local participatory health development planning.

These strategic axes will be carried out with all stakeholders in an incremental, gradual process described by Lindblom (5) and a mixed top-down and bottom-up process described by Sabatier (6).

Conclusion and recommendations

The operationalization of deconcentration and devolution in the health sector is a complex process that must be implemented in an incremental, gradual, participatory, mixed manner combining top-down and bottom-up approaches, taking into account the interests of the various stakeholders. It requires intelligent collaboration between the deconcentrated services of the Ministry of Health and local governments through a largely participatory planning process and consensual coordination of health activities at the local level.

Key words: Health decentralization, devolution, skills transfer, policy.

LIST OF ABBREVIATIONS AND ACRONYMS

ARDCI	Assembly of Regions and Districts of Côte d'Ivoire
BM	World Bank
CHU	University Hospital
CIADD	Interministerial Support Unit for Deconcentration-Devolution
CT	Territorial Authority
DDS	Departmental Health Directorate
DPPEIS	Department of Foresight, Planning, Evaluation and Health Information
HRD	Human Resources Department
DRS	Regional Health Department
ECD	District Executive Team
ENV	Household Living Standards Survey
EPN	National Public Establishment
ERS	Regional Health Team
CWSF	First Contact Health Facility
IMF	International Monetary Fund
GAR	Results-Based Management
GC	Central Government
GL	Local Government
INSP	National Institute of Public Health
MEF	Ministry of Economy and Finance
MEMIS	Ministry of State Ministry of the Interior and Security
MFP	Ministry of the Civil Service
MSHP	Ministry of Health and Public Hygiene
NPSP	New Public Health Pharmacy
WHO	World Health Organization
NGO	Non-Governmental Organization
PEPFAR	President's Emergency Plan for AIDS Relief
PMA	care activity packages
PND	National Development Plan
PNDS	National Health Development Plan
UNDP	United Nations Development Programme
PRDS	Regional Health Development Plan
PTF	Technical and Financial Partner
SNIS	National Health Information System

SSP   Primary Health Care
USAID   United States Agency for International Development
UVICOCI   Union of Cities and Towns of Côte d'Ivoire

1 Introduction

The decline of the welfare state due to the global economic crisis caused by the oil crisis of the 1970s and 1980s led to a shift in the modes of administration and management of many countries in the world towards decentralization (7). A partnership solution was found with the territorial State, which is a combination of the State and the local authorities to ensure harmonious local development (8). While the evidence that the management of public goods at a level closer to the citizens would better respond to their needs is still very nuanced (9).

Decentralization is a system of management in which powers are conferred on an entity that is separate from the central administration. It is a management method that consists in bringing decision-making power closer to the population and services closer to the users(1). Decentralization is also a choice and a political, administrative and financial strategy of organization and management to ensure the development of a national territory (9). It has been adopted by many countries throughout the world for reasons of efficiency, rationality and reactivity due to the proximity of decision-making power, the speed of decision-making and the permanent contact between citizens and leaders (2). Accompanied by capacity building of local actors, community participation and transfer of power, decentralization is supposed to accelerate the evolution towards community empowerment to ensure sustainable local development (3).

Many low- and middle-income countries have suffered the consequences of the oil crisis and the global economic crisis that it generated. Among the reforms adopted to remedy this situation is decentralization, for the reasons mentioned above, but also in order to benefit from development aid from the Bretton Woods institutions such as the World Bank and the International Monetary Fund (IMF).

Côte d'Ivoire, which has not escaped this wave of reform, contains the four forms of decentralization described by Rondinelli, namely deconcentration, delegation, devolution and privatization (7). However, in the conduct of the decentralization process, emphasis is placed on two types, namely deconcentration and devolution, which have been described in the various legislative and regulatory texts (laws, decrees, etc.) (10,11).
- **Deconcentration** is the bringing of the central level closer to the periphery. The Ministry of Health comes closer to the population through its deconcentrated services (regional directorates and health districts) which have no autonomy but depend on the central level for all actions (4,7).
- **Devolution** is the transfer of power or competencies and means from the State to the authorities elected by the people to whom they are accountable. These are the Territorial

Communities (TCs), also called local governments (LGs), which are the regions and municipalities. The management bodies (Regional and Municipal Councils) work in complete autonomy (4,7).

Our work has therefore focused on how to get these two administrations, decentralized services of the Ministry of Health and local governments, to work together, in intelligent collaboration, harmonizing their actions to improve the health of their constituents. It is not a question of merging the two administrations but of strengthening collaboration between them for a progressive transfer of health competencies to local governments. This collaboration, which we have called the **coupling of deconcentration and devolution** or the **deconcentration-devolution policy** throughout this work, is also achieved through a process of participatory and consensual planning and coordination of health activities at the local level to improve the supply of health services and care to the population.

2 Rationale for the study

The Ministry of Health has a department called the Department of Foresight, Planning, Evaluation and Health Information (DPPEIS) whose mission is to contribute to the operationalization of deconcentration and devolution in health. Thus, the DPPEIS, which is the department in which I work, has undertaken several actions including participatory planning of health development under the leadership of the Regional Council. All of these actions have been carried out to involve and engage the deconcentrated services and local governments in the process of transferring and distributing health competencies from the State to local governments. In fact, several texts, including "Law No. 2003-208 of July 7, 2003, on the transfer and distribution of competencies from the State to the local governments" (11), have been adopted by the State to make devolution effective in all sectors, including health.

The problem is that despite the adoption of various texts, and the initiatives of the Ministry of Health, the local devolved administrations are struggling to work in harmony for the health of local populations. Local governments have difficulty in taking over the competencies to exercise them in accordance with the texts and directives established in this area, for various reasons that undermine this important reform for the Ivorian health system.

These reasons which were also sources of difficulties during our activities are :

- the inadequacy, incompleteness and unsuitability of the institutional and legal framework for decentralization and the transfer of competencies from the State to the Territorial Communities;

- the mismatch between the territorial administrative division and the health administrative division;

- the absence or insufficiency of transfer of means to the Territorial Collectivities;

- the absence of a policy document on health decentralization and a strategy for the implementation

implementation of the process of transfer and appropriation of health competences by the Territorial Communities.

All of this is taking place in a context of recurrent political and military crises and institutional instability that the country experienced from 1999 to 2011. This situation is reflected on the ground in the fragmentation of planning and coordination of local health activities, weak accountability mechanisms and quality of care, and inefficiency of health action.

Our research question is that, given the devolution process underway in the health sector in Côte d'Ivoire, how can we operationalize the combination of deconcentration and devolution by strengthening the planning and coordination system at the local level, given the fragmentation of health action?

Our hypothesis is that participatory and consensual planning and coordination of health activities at the local level, between the deconcentrated services of the Ministry of Health and local governments, could contribute to strengthening the coupling of deconcentration and devolution and to improving the supply of health services and care to the population.

3 Objectives

3.1 General objective

The general objective of our study is to contribute to the operationalization of devolution and deconcentration by strengthening the planning and coordination system of health activities at the local level.

3.2 Specific objectives

The specific objectives are:

1. Analyze the current organization and evolution of deconcentration and devolution in the health sector in Côte d'Ivoire

2. Describe how the implementation of the health planning process at the local level could improve devolution and deconcentration in the health sector

3. Propose solutions to operationalize the local planning process in the health sector in Côte d'Ivoire.

4 Literature review

In this section, we will review the relevant literature on decentralization in general, and then in the health sector in low- and middle-income countries in particular.

4.1 Theoretical and conceptual framework

The purpose of this chapter is to trace the origins of our study and place it in a theoretical and conceptual framework by reviewing the literature on the concepts of decentralization in general and decentralization in the health sector in particular.

1)   Description of the concepts of decentralization

> **Rondinelli**

Decentralization has been described by Rondinelli according to four types: deconcentration, delegation, devolution and privatization (7).

Deconcentration can be defined as a dismemberment of the central level towards the periphery. For example, the Ministry of Health is represented or brought closer to the population through its regional and departmental health directorates called health districts (4). These structures are the units that operationalize the policies defined at the central level through the implementation of essential packages of activities. They are directly monitored, supervised, controlled and evaluated regularly with a readjustment of the activity packages by the central level (7).

Delegation can be defined as a transfer of responsibility and authority to semi-autonomous structures (4) that are only indirectly controlled by the central level (7). In Côte d'Ivoire, in the health sector, responsibilities have been delegated to semi-autonomous parastatals called Etablissements Publics Nationaux (EPN). These EPNs include the University Hospital Centers (CHU), the New Public Health Pharmacy (NPSP) which is the central purchasing and distribution center for drugs, etc. However, the ultimate responsibility lies with the Ministry of Health (7).

Devolution can be defined as a transfer of power or competencies and means (12) to authorities elected by the people to whom they are accountable, leading to more democratic governance (3). For example, the transfer of authority and responsibility for health to local authorities such as regions, communes and autonomous districts in Côte d'Ivoire.

Privatization can be defined as the granting of responsibilities, functions, and sometimes assets to non-public actors, often with an agreement to determine the role that is expected in return (4). For example, the Ministry of Health grants authorizations to non-governmental organizations (NGOs), faith-based organizations, companies, etc., to open private health facilities and exercise operational responsibilities in health (7).

Figure 1: Illustration of the decentralized health administration system in Côte d'Ivoire

Source: adapted from Rondinelli (1983) (7)

As Figure 1 above shows, in Côte d'Ivoire there is a combination of all the forms of decentralization, according to Rondinelli's categorization, each of which coexists in its own sphere of competence. Similarly, in each country there is always a combination of all these typologies in

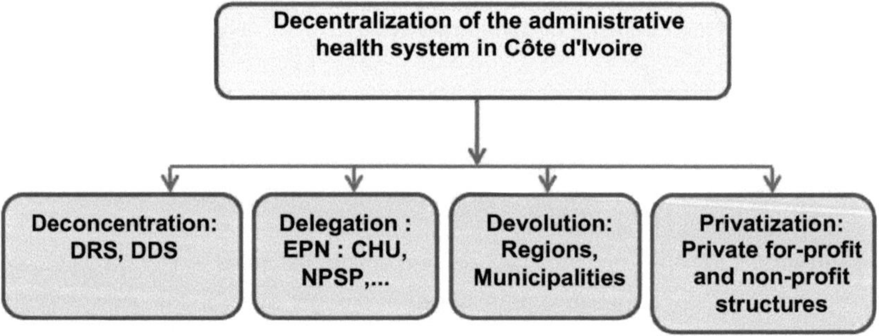

different proportions.

The strengths of this typology described by Rondinelli is the ease of observation and identification of the powers received or lost by the different institutional entities (4). According to Bossert, the aspects to be improved in this approach lie in the fact that it does not provide enough elements to explore the responsibilities that are transferred from one organizational entity to another and does not allow for the identification of the diversity and scope of the decision-making spaces that are available to central and local stakeholders(4). According to Gilson, "it does not provide us with analytical tools to specify and compare tasks and functions" (13) and does not consider decentralization as a dynamic process.

> **Litvack**

Litvack (1998) has also developed a different categorization of decentralization as "political, administrative, financial and market decentralization" (14).

Political decentralization, often linked to political pluralism or multipartyism and representative government, can support democratization by giving citizens or their elected representatives more influence in the formulation and execution of a country's policy.

Administrative decentralization, which takes three of the four forms analyzed by Rondinelli, namely deconcentration, delegation and devolution (14).

Decentralization of finance, which emphasizes the transfer of resources, sources of funding, and financial resources for local governments and private organizations to carry out their functions, as well as the power to make decisions about expenditures. Revenues at a level appropriate to the competencies of the Local Government, either from local sources or from a transfer from the central government. This may include cost recovery, co-financing, taxation, inter-governmental transfers and authorizations for local governments to borrow, etc. (14).

Economic or market decentralization, which deals with privatization and deregulation sometimes accompanied by economic liberalization and market development policies. They allow functions that were primarily or exclusively the responsibility of government to be performed by the private sector, communities, cooperatives, private voluntary associations, and other nongovernmental organizations (14).

The strength of this thematic analysis is that it takes into account and goes beyond the description made by Rondinelli. It allows us to explore the scope of certain responsibilities and decision-making spaces (political, economic and financial) that are within the reach of central and local actors. The difficulty with this typology of decentralization lies in the overlapping meanings of certain terms and the diversity of forms it can take in different countries or within the same sector (14).

2)   Theory of decentralization in low and middle income countries

>   The concept of the Bossert decision space

Political scientist Thomas Bossert uses several analytical concepts on decentralization issues, namely (i) public administration, (ii) local fiscal choice, (iii) social capital and (iv) the principal agent approach (4). He has also used his "decision space" framework in several comparative studies of decentralization systems (15-18).

Bossert examines the impact of restricting or enlarging "decision spaces" for different themes (financing, organization of services, human resources and governance). In addition, he studies the modes of governance or policies available at the central level to influence these choices (4).

According to J. Mohammed (2016), the approach developed by Bossert allows for an assessment of the degree of decentralization based on the transfer of decision-making. The "decision space" tool, which proposes to examine the sphere of decision making in the four typologies of decentralization, is appropriate because it allows for the examination of the dynamic and evolving relationship between the central and the local as a result of decentralization (12). He argues that the approach used by Bossert is appropriate for its applicability to low- and middle-income countries (12). However, a notable criticism of this tool is that it is a formal map of the decision space that may not reflect the actual scope of decisions that the agent may have in countries where laws are not enforced or are easily violated by the agent (12). Another limitation is that Bossert's framework only gives a view of the decision space of the local level vis-à-vis the central level but does not analyze the local fabric and capabilities at the local level (9).

> **Brinkerhoff's concept of community empowerment and decentralization in fragile states**

In this earlier work, Brinkerhoff examines how bringing power closer to the people, or returning decision-making power to the people, could help expand democracy and strengthen the quality of health service delivery (3). Later, he studied the relationship between decentralization in fragile states, democratic governance, and citizens' perceptions of the state (19). According to Brinkerhoff (2006), decentralization can help improve community participation in order to empower the population. The autonomous population can make its own choices, not only for its health, education, agricultural and other needs, but also for its local and national governors (3). An assumption often used to justify the initiation of the decentralization process in developing countries.

According to Brinkerhoff (2009), local democratic space is strongly influenced by the distribution of authority at the local level (9). Systems with strong mayors and weak city councils have limited democracy compared to systems that balance authority more evenly between mayors and councils, and that involve citizens in council meetings. He emphasizes issues of inclusiveness and participation, arguing that deepening democracy requires the active engagement in public affairs of citizens from all socio-economic strata. He warns of the risk of resource capture by local elites, which must be addressed and measures taken to correct this (9).

Regarding empowerment, Brinkerhoff explains that "in countries with weak civil societies or in post-conflict situations where societies have deep socio-ethnic cleavages, the capacity for collective action within a community is likely to be fragile and easily broken by internal mistrust or by the external actions of state actors to exert control" (divide and conquer) (3). It is unrealistic to expect that a large number of individuals will necessarily be interested in collective action from the outset (ex ante). It is therefore more reasonable to assume that a small number of community representatives are initially engaged, acting on behalf of their communities. Autonomous individuals can make significant progress on a collective agenda, even in some cases stimulating an encouraged minority to advocate on behalf of their community (9).

Drawing on the literature, he defines community empowerment operationally in terms of four elements. Communities are empowered if they:

- have access to information,
- are not excluded but take part in forums where problems are discussed and decisions are made,
- can hold decision makers accountable for their choices and actions, and
- have the capacity and means to organize and articulate their interests and assume roles as partners with public service delivery agencies (3).

Some governments may continue their efforts to increase empowerment and decentralization because they believe it is in their interest to do so, and therefore will be strengthened (9). Conversely, governments that perceive little to gain from increased openness, transparency and direct citizen participation will be less likely to support empowerment efforts. As with any reform, entrenched interests that benefit from the current institutional environment will resist changes, for example, to expand the set of rights available to citizens and to put in place mechanisms to empower communities. Dealing with resistance to local levelling requires political will and proactive intervention from the center (3).

4.2 Decentralization and development aid

Decentralization started for most African countries during the colonial period (Mali, Niger, Senegal, Ivory Coast,...). At independence, Senegal already had thirty-four fully-fledged communes. In Mali, too, thirteen urban communes were created during colonization (20), and Côte d'Ivoire contained three full-fledged communes and rural communes without real powers.

The end of the welfare state brought about by the global economic crisis of the 1980s, coupled with the World Bank's Structural Adjustment Plan and the conditioning of foreign aid, prompted central governments to reduce their interference in the social sectors. This led to the strengthening of decentralization in African countries in the 1980s and 1990s. This requirement was legitimized by the inability of the state to manage the country effectively and equitably from the central level, to mitigate such ills as mismanagement, lack of equity in development, service delivery and infrastructure.

In ordor to ensure that aid actually reaches citizens, some donors do not hesitate to bypass governments to deal with the local level (9). Decentralization can help stabilize society and build citizens' confidence in their ability to choose their political leaders and hold them accountable (9). Through decentralization, states, through local governments, could easily assume the governance functions described by Brinkerhoff, including security, provision of basic public services, community participation and public sector accountability (21).

As a result, decentralization was accelerated in the 2000s by the political will of certain African political leaders who wrote it into their new constitutions and laws to ensure territorial reorganization and give more power to local governments. These local governments, with financial and management autonomy, are led by a deliberative assembly elected by universal suffrage (20). However, the lack of real political commitment has not allowed the implementation of these reforms to translate this political will into reality on the ground.

4.3 Decentralization and public health

The first decades following the independence of the Ivory Coast, like many African states, were marked by a very centralized public health policy. This policy consisted essentially of the creation of hospitals, dispensaries and maternity wards in the cities, as well as the creation of mobile services for the control of major endemic diseases in the villages and countryside, all in favor of the economic upturn (22).

However, during the 1980s, events such as the severe economic and financial crisis led the country to hybridize its centralized policy with touches of decentralization. Then, Côte d'Ivoire adopted the Alma Ata declaration on primary health care (PHC) which emphasized community participation (23). In addition, there is pressure from the World Bank and the IMF to reduce the presence of the state in the social sectors and favor private initiatives. All these events have accelerated the policy of deconcentration in public health for the implementation of primary health care. The country therefore undertook reforms of the health system with the creation of regional health directorates in 1985, the implementation of the Bamako Initiative in 1992, with the practice of cost recovery of health care procedures within public establishments and the creation of health districts in 1994. It also defined packages of care activities (PMA) at the level of the regions and health districts in 1996 (24) and adopted the first national health development plan (PNDS) 1996-2005 in which it aimed to improve access to health services and promote primary health care (PHC) (25). At the same time, starting in the 1980s, the government strengthened the communalization of the country and local elected officials began to take an interest in the health problems of their citizens by building health centers, which they then entrusted to the Ministry of Health to put into operation. In addition, as in many African countries, the public sector did not have exclusive responsibility for health, since there was not only a private health sector but also a large non-governmental (faith-based) sector whose administrative structure was often highly decentralized and located in areas sometimes far from the capital (26).

Despite all these initiatives, decentralization in the health sector is still far from being effective because neither the transfer of competencies nor the transfer of resources is real. There is a big gap between what is written in the texts and the reality on the ground.

4.4 Planning and capacity building of local actors

1) Planning

Decentralization, particularly devolution in the health sector, suggests a transfer of powers, competencies and resources from the State represented by the Ministry of Health to the local government accountable to the people who elected it. However, can we be sure of the capacity of local actors to ensure these new functions?

One of the objectives of decentralization is to bring power and decision-making closer to the people and to encourage community participation. But this presupposes that the country has enough competent managers to fill the technical positions in order to carry out the functions transferred. In addition, in the face of this plethora of administrations, there must be a great capacity for internal and external coordination with other local governments, but above all a great capacity at the central level to ensure coordination of the entire process (26). This coordination can be achieved through a bottom-up planning process. Indeed, planning can be a powerful tool for coordinating activities at the local level between the deconcentrated services of the Ministry of Health and local governments. But only if this planning is participatory, mixed, mainly bottom-up but also top-down, equitable, taking into account the diversity of opinion, minorities and gender, and implemented in a participatory and consensual manner. Only then can planning contribute to better coordination of activities at the peripheral level.

2) Capacity building of local actors

According to Brinkerhoff & Azfar (2006), the argument of incompetence of local actors should not be put forward against the devolution process because it "creates institutional arenas where citizens learn democratic skills   . The devolution with the transfer of competences and means to local governments can therefore be considered as a springboard for local actors to learn, to increase their competences, knowledge, know-how and skills in all sectors of activity including health (9).

In addition, the experience gained by local actors could enable policy entrepreneurs and reformers to sharpen their strategies and other tactics for pushing through and implementing reforms in different sectors, especially health. Brinkerhoff & Johnson (2009) give the example of Rwanda where "the Ministry of Territorial Administration encourages local authorities to experiment with administrative and service delivery options. These experiments are rewarded in a national competition for local government awards, and promising innovations are labeled as best practices and some are replicated in other regions" (9).

He adds that community empowerment tools such as participatory planning and budgeting provide opportunities for community leaders and locally elected officials to develop skills and experience in public debate, advocacy, local organizational capacity building and coalition building (3).

In sum, bottom-up participatory planning contributes to capacity building of local actors and to better coordination of actions at the local level. It is essential for good collaboration between deconcentrated services and local governments in the context of the operationalization of the deconcentration-devolution couple.

5 Methodology

The methodology describes the research strategy, the design of the study, the method of data collection and analysis, and the types of documents used for the analysis, as well as the reliability and validity of the data.

5.1 Design (type of study)

The Design or type of study is a single holistic case study.

The case is the coupling of deconcentration and devolution through the regional health development planning process, in the context of Côte d'Ivoire. This is the process of developing Regional Health Development Plans (PRDS).

The case study was used in this work for the three reasons mentioned by Lucy Gilson(27). First, it is flexible and adaptable to the specificity of the dynamic and changing context in which our study is situated. Second, it allows us to study the complex and evolving positions of stakeholders and institutions and the interactions between them. Finally, with the case study we can, at the same time as we analyze the planning process, make recommendations for practical implementation in the health sector in Côte d'Ivoire.

5.2 Research strategy

This was an exploratory study that used mixed quantitative and qualitative secondary data. Having worked for seven years in the field of health decentralization as an official in the Ministry of Health, we drew on our personal experience and knowledge, exploited authorized documents from the Ministry of Health and the Ministry in charge of Administration and other technical ministries. The study also relied on data from various national and international documents and information sources through a review of the English and French literature using the search engines Medline (pubmed), Google Scholar and the online databases of the Institute of Tropical Medicine (ITM) and other regional research institutes (CODESRIA, LASDEL, etc.) with key words (policy, decentralization, devolution, transfer of competencies, health) in order to describe the situation, to establish our problem and to elaborate the results and analyses. The research strategy is detailed in Appendix 1.

5.3 Data collection

Quantitative and qualitative data were collected through several distinct sources.

On the website of the General Directorate of Decentralization and Local Development (DGDDL) of the Ministry of State, Ministry of the Interior and Security (MEMIS), referred to in our work as the Ministry in charge of Territorial Administration, we have downloaded the relevant texts, namely laws, ordinances, decrees and orders, in relation to our study

We also explored data provided by the National Health Information System (SNIS), evaluation documents, policies and strategies developed in health. In addition, international reports such as those of the WHO, WB, UNDP, etc. were consulted.

The reports of the activities and missions we conducted in the field, published and unpublished research reports, and grey literature on decentralization in the health sector in Côte d'Ivoire were also explored.

In Google Scholar and online library databases, the keywords we used for the search were:
- "Decentralization health;
- "Transfer of skills" and "Transfer of skills" and
- The term "health policy" or "policy health" is used to refer to the health policy of a country.

For Medline (PubMed), where possible, the MeSH terms that were used were "Decentralization", "health", "policy", "devolution", "Decentralization health", "policy health", "Transfer skills".

From this combination: **(((((Health) AND Policy)) AND Decentralization)) AND ((Devolution) OR ((transfer) AND skills))** we obtained 59 articles in Medeline. The raw results of the Medline (PubMed) and Google Scholar search are detailed in Appendix 2.

Several searches were conducted with various combinations of keywords in order to reach as many articles as possible. The results of the search were recorded in Mendeley reference manager to build the bibliography of our work. Additional literature was retrieved by a "snowball effect" from the bibliography of key articles found.

5.3.1 Selection of studies

> Inclusion criteria

Articles, reports, documents, and grey literature dealing with decentralization in general and decentralization in the health sector in particular were included in the study. Emphasis was placed on literature from low- and middle-income countries, particularly from Africa.

> Exclusion Criteria

Articles and other papers that did not deal with decentralization, as well as those that dealt with it exclusively in high-income countries, were excluded. We also excluded studies written in languages other than English and French. Details of the selection of the 22 studies used for the review and analysis of the results are provided in Appendix 3: Flowchart search results. These studies were supplemented by forty other literatures and documents to reach the sixty-two documents in the bibliography.

5.4 Methods of data analysis

Conceptual frameworks were adapted and used to guide data compilation and analysis. Thus, we adapted and used theories and policy analysis frameworks to analyze the process of deconcentration and devolution in health in Côte d'Ivoire. We conducted an in-depth analysis of devolution using a framework adapted from Brinkerhoff (2006), combining the decision space developed by Bossert (1998) and community empowerment described by Brinkerhoff (2006) (3). We described the historical process and contextual analysis with the framework of Leichter in Walt, 1994 (28). Stakeholder analysis was conducted using the framework of Johnson & Scholes, 2002 (29). Implementation was studied through the incremental theory of Lindblom, 1959 (5). The type of governance was analyzed with the framework of Van Belle, 2016 (30,31), and the mode of governance with Bell, 2009 and Sorensen, 2009 (32,33).

5.5 Validity and reliability of data

This work was based on literature reviews and related studies and findings. We used triangulation to ensure data quality, confirmability and transferability of results. In addition, during the analysis of the data, we constantly used the conceptual frameworks to guide the synthesis of the respective results, without omitting the analysis of negative cases, in order to improve the reliability of the data and their credibility.

5.6 Ethical considerations

We have used documents from the public domain and professional documents authorized by the Ministry of Health and the Ministry of Territorial Administration and have referenced each source for intellectual honesty.

6 Results and analysis

In Côte d'Ivoire, among the four categories of decentralization, the operationalization of the decentralization process, has focused on two types which are deconcentration with regional directorates and health districts and devolution with local governments (LG). It is not a question of merging them because the current law (No. 2014-451 of August 05, 2014) provides for the existence of the two local health and territorial administrations, each evolving in its sphere of competence (10). Our work has therefore focused on the coupling of deconcentration and devolution which is the way to bring these two administrations to work in a collegial way. The study focused on the participatory planning process, which is a suitable mechanism for the consensual coordination of health activities.

The results of our study can be divided into three main parts.

The first part or descriptive analysis of the implementation of the deconcentration-devolution coupling process is presented in three points which are:

- context analysis with the adapted Leichter framework (28).
- analysis of the historical process and content since the independence of the Ivory Coast, using the framework adapted from Walt & Gilson, 1994 (34) and summarized by the timeline;
- stakeholder analysis using the Johnson & Scholes, 2002 framework (29).

The second part consisted of an in-depth analysis of the decentralization and devolution pair using a framework adapted from Brinkerhoff (2006), combining the decision space developed by Bossert (1998) and the empowerment of communities described by Brinkerhoff (2006) (3).

Finally, the third part consisted in analyzing the planning process as one of the mechanisms for implementing the policy of decentralization-devolution coupling in health.

6.1 Descriptive analysis of the implementation of the deconcentration and devolution policy

1- Context of Côte d'Ivoire

Côte d'Ivoire is a country located in West Africa, covering an area of 322,462 km^2 and has 22,671,331 inhabitants with a density of 70.3 inhabitants/km^2 (35).
The results of the contextual analysis conducted with the framework adapted from Leichter in walt,

1994 (28), are summarized in Table 1 below.

Table 1: Results of the contextual analysis with the framework of Leichter in walt, 1994

Situational factors	Fragile state: since 1999 successive socio-political and military crises, political, security and institutional instability Weakness of health indicators (see Table 3)
Socio-cultural factors	Low and unequal literacy rate: men (53.3%), women (36.3%) Poverty index at 46.3% higher in rural areas (56.8%) than in urban areas (35.9%) Inequity in local development, regional disparity
Exogenous factors	Economy influenced by global raw material costs High dependence on international aid conditioned on investment High presence of non-nationals, who represent 24.2% of the total population
Structural factors	Weak accountability mechanisms Precarious political, security and economic stability Poor redistribution of resources, mistrust between peoples

Source: Adapted from Leichter in walt, 1994 (28)

At the administrative level, Table 2 below shows that the health division is not superimposed on the administrative division, a disharmony that is sometimes a source of discrepancy. See also Annex 4 for maps of administrative and health regions.

Tableau 2   Summary of the administrative and health territorial organization

Deconcentration		Devolution
Administrative division	**Sanitary division**	**Local authorities**
31 Regions	20 health regions	31 Regions
108 Departments	83 departments or health districts	197 Municipalities
510 Sub-prefectures		
>8600 Villages		
02 Autonomous Districts (Abidjan and Yamoussoukro) both devolved and devolved		

Source: Law n°2014-451 05 August 2014 and Order n°007/MSLS/CAB 02 February 2012 (10,36)

In terms of social and health care, maternal and neonatal morbidity and mortality remain high and worrying in Côte d'Ivoire. Table 3 below summarizes some key socio-health indicators.

Tableau 3   Social and Health Indicators

Indicators	Data
Maternal mortality ratio	614/100000 live births
Neonatal mortality	38/1000 live births
Infant and child mortality rate	108/1000 live births

Life expectancy at birth (years)	53,1
Gross Domestic Product ($)	31.76 billion
GDP growth rate (%)	9,2
Human Development Index (HDI, 2014)	0.452 (ranked 171ème State out of 187)

Source: DHS-MICS 2011-2012, World Bank, UNDP(37-39)

This background is the by-product of a tumultuous history described in the next point.

2- Historical context

> Start of the decentralization policy

Figure 2: Timeline of the evolution of decentralization policy in Côte d'Ivoire

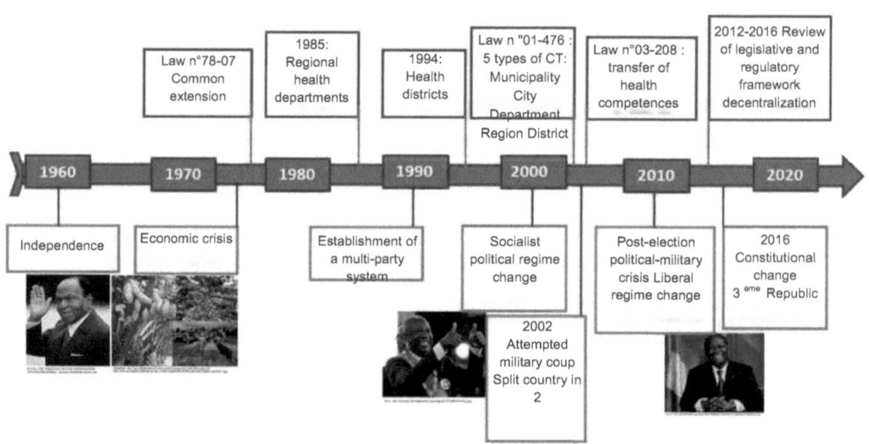

Source: author, 2017

As the timeline in Figure 2 above indicates, in Côte d'Ivoire, the policy of decentralization dates back to independence in 1960 under the presidency of Félix Houphouët Boigny, who initially created three full-fledged communes: Grand-Bassam, Abidjan and Bouaké. From the 1980s onwards, decentralization was accentuated: - in its devolved form by the extension of communes to twenty-eight and

- in its deconcentration form in the health sector, with the creation of regional and district health directorates in 1985 and 1994 respectively.

- Deepening of the decentralization policy

The policy of deconcentration-devolution gained momentum from 2000 onwards with the accession to power of President Laurent Gbagbo, a socialist politician. He moved from a simple desire to a strong political commitment by passing several laws, including "Law n°2001-476 of 9 August 2001 on the general organization of territorial administration" (40). According to this law, the deconcentrated territorial administration comprises four types of administrative districts with hierarchical links between them (see Table 2, page 18). These are:

- regions headed by regional prefects,
- the departments under the direction of the departmental prefects,
- the sub-prefectures led by the sub-prefects and
- villages led by village chiefs.

These administrative districts are headed by authorities appointed by the central administration. The weakness of these administrative officials is that their sense of accountability is more oriented towards their superiors who appointed them or nominated them for appointment to the detriment of the people they are supposed to serve. Many of them are more interested in satisfying their superiors in order to retain their positions rather than responding to the needs of the people.

The law also created, within the framework of devolution, five types of Territorial Authorities without hierarchical links between them and with legal personality and financial autonomy (40). These are the regions, departments, districts, cities and municipalities, which are governed by authorities elected directly by the people for a renewable five-year term (41). The governing bodies of these local governments are summarized in Table 4 below.

Table 4: Summary of governing bodies of local authorities

Type of local authority	Deliberative body	Executive support body	Executive Authority	Collegial advisory body
Municipality	City Council	Municipality	Mayor of the commune	none
City	City Council	Municipality	Mayor of the city	none
Department	Council General	General Council Office	President of the General Council	Departmental Economic and Social Committee
District	District Council	District Council Office	District Governor	District Advisory Committee
Region	Council Regional	Regional Council Office	President of the Regional Council	Regional Economic and Social Committee

Source: Law n°2001- 476 of August 9, 2001 (40)

The missions of the governing bodies are:

the organization of the collective life ;
the participation of the population in the management of local affairs;

- the promotion and realization of local development;
- modernization of the rural world ;
- the improvement of the living environment; the management of the land and the environment.

However, starting in September 2002, Côte d'Ivoire experienced an attempted coup d'état, which turned into an armed rebellion that split the country into two zones, the south under government control and the central, northern and western zones (CNO) under the control of the armed rebellion (see Annex 5 where the government zone is in pink, in the south) (42). This political-military crisis created institutional instability and weakened the country. Despite these unfortunate events, the process of deconcentration and devolution continued in 2003, leading to the adoption of "Law n°2003-208 of July 7, 2003 on the transfer and distribution of competencies from the State to the Territorial Collectivities. It devolved competencies in sixteen areas, including health, to local governments (see Annex 6) (11).

- **Health competencies transferred to local governments**

In the area of health, there are four types of competencies that have been divided among the five types of Local Governments (summarized in Annex 7). Thus, all local governments can:
- Develop and implement a health development plan, consistent with the community's plan;
- to give their opinion on the prospective development of the national health map;
- adopt preventive measures in the field of health, public hygiene and
food.
- The fourth competence, which is the construction, management and maintenance of health facilities, is exercised differently depending on the type of local authority and the type of health facility. As a result :
- the region, through the Regional Council, builds, manages and maintains the regional hospitals (secondary care hospitals);
- The department, through the general council, builds, manages and maintains the general hospitals (primary care hospitals);
- The district and the city, respectively through the district council and the city council, build, manage and maintain general hospitals and public health and food establishments;
- the municipality, through the municipal council, builds, manages and maintains the health centers or Primary Health Care Facilities (PHCF) (11).

- **Competencies held by the Ministry of Health**

The competences still held by the Ministry of Health and executed by its central and deconcentrated services are
- to define and implement the national policy on health, public hygiene and quality;
- to elaborate, follow and control the application of the national health development plan and the national health map;
- to elaborate the framework of the initiatives of the Territorial Communities in the field of health;
- to approve the health plans and programs of the Territorial Communities;
- Approve curricula for health education and training institutions;

- to determine the standards and procedures for the siting, construction, rehabilitation, equipment, opening, organization, operation and management of health facilities;
- managing health information;
- manage health care staff ;
- ensure the response to epidemics and major health disasters.

The shortcoming of this policy is that it was initiated top-down by the Presidency of the Republic and the Ministry in charge of Territorial Administration. Despite the adoption of these texts, the frequent twists and turns in the political-military crisis that weakened the country from 1999 to 2011, with its attendant governmental and institutional instability, have made it difficult to apply the texts initiated by President Laurent Gbagbo. The inherent economic difficulties, the large internal displacements of the population, and the growing mistrust between the people have put a brake on the implementation of the deconcentration-devolution policy.

- **Degradation of social and health indicators**

At the health level, the decree for the application of the law has not been issued to specify the modalities for its implementation, leading to a disruption in the implementation of the deconcentration-devolution policy. The deconcentrated health services and local governments work separately, resulting in fragmented coordination and planning, which makes health action inefficient.

The basic health indicators (see Tables 1 and 3, pages 17 and 18) have therefore deteriorated to levels that are worrying in view of expectations. Indeed, maternal and neonatal morbidity and mortality as well as the poverty index remain high and worrying in Côte d'Ivoire (43,44).
The consequences of the successive crises that the country has experienced and the fragmentation of the health action could explain this underperformance. These are particularly :
- Discontinuity in policy implementation due to institutional instability with frequent changes in the Ministry of Health;
- the massive migration and demobilization of human resources fleeing the central, northern and western zones occupied by the rebellion, thus aggravating the problem of inequity in their distribution;
- Decreased technical and financial support for health development;
- the weak capacity for planning, coordination, management, monitoring and evaluation of health action at the macro, meso and micro levels of the health system;
- the progressive depredation of the operational capacities of local actors (42).

This politico-military crisis ended in a post-electoral crisis in 2010-2011 with the accession to power of President Alassane Ouattara of liberal political persuasion in April 2011. He reiterated the political will to pursue the policy of deconcentration-devolution by revising the texts taken by the previous regime and by developing new texts to improve the ongoing process.

3- Current policy

Law n°2003-208 of July 7, 2003 on the transfer and distribution of powers from the State to the Territorial Collectivities" (11) transfers health powers to five categories of local governments. At present, some texts have been revised, including the "law n° 2014-451 of August 5, 2014 on the orientation of the general organization of the Territorial Administration" which abolished three categories of local governments to keep only the Regional Council (region) and the Municipal Council (commune) (10). The 2003 law on the transfer of powers has therefore become obsolete and needs to be readapted. However, its revision is dragging on because of disagreements between the various stakeholders, of which our analysis has focused on the most important ones using the adapted Johnson and Scholes framework (29). The details of this analysis are in Appendices 8 and 9.

The limitation of the framework used, as with most frameworks, is that it is a snapshot in a dynamic, rapidly changing environment. There is potential for changes in stakeholder positions, interests, alliances, and influences over time. If the position of one actor changes, the positions of others are likely to change and the political context for decision-making is often unstable.

The current policy of deconcentration-devolution, which began when President Ouattara came to power, is based on the presidential program entitled "Vivre ensemble" (45).

It has several objectives including:

- the anchoring of local democracy ;
- the correction of local inequalities and a better distribution of the fruits of the growth;
- the promotion of local development and good governance (45).

The implementation of this new policy was planned to take place in three major consecutive phases: the start-up phase, the ramp-up phase and the cruising phase.

First phase or start-up phase

It consisted in the institutional, territorial, strategic and legal framing through some following activities:

- the adoption of law n°2014-451 of 5 August 2014 on the general organization of territorial administration, which repealed law n°2001-476 of 9 August 2001. It laid the foundations of territorial administration through deconcentration, which retained the four categories of administrative districts (region, department, sub-prefecture and village) and devolution, which abolished three types of Territorial Collectivities (department, district, town) to move from five to two types of Territorial Collectivities which are the region and the commune (10).
- the adoption of decree n°2011-263 of 28 September 2011 on the organization of the national

territory into districts and regions, supplemented by decree n°2012-612 of 04 July 2012 on the creation of the Moronou region, which creates thirty-one Territorial Collectivities or local governments (46,47).
-   the abolition by decree dated March 7, 2012 of the 1,126 Communes created between 2001 and 2010, pending the definition of the new framework for the total communalization of the national territory.
-   the adoption of law n°2012-1128 of 13 December 2012 on the organization of the Territorial Collectivities (41).
-   the organization of combined municipal and regional elections in April 2013 and the effective installation of regional councils.
-   the adoption of decrees n°2013-486 and n°2013-487 of July 11, 2013 setting the rules for decentralized cooperation and establishing, organizing and operating the national committee for decentralized cooperation.

The unfinished activities of this phase are the adoption of complementary texts to the previous ones, including
-   the new configuration of the transfer and distribution of competences from the State to the Territorial Collectivities;
-   the reform of the status of the personnel of the Local Authorities;
-   the reform of the financial, fiscal and property regime of the Local Authorities.

Second phase or ramp-up phase
It consisted in implementing the projects contained in the NDP 2016-2020 in relation to deconcentration-devolution that should contribute to the country's progress towards emergence in 2020. These projects can be summarized as follows:
-   the preparation of a national policy framework document on deconcentration and devolution;
-   the adaptation and modernization of the financial management and accounting rules of the Local Authorities;
-   capacity building of the actors of deconcentration-devolution ;
-   the creation of a municipal development agency providing technical support to local authorities;
-   the reform of the loan fund for local authorities and its transformation into a development bank for local authorities;
-   the creation of the Institute for Capacity Building of Local Authorities and its transformation into a university of local authorities;
-   the development and implementation of a communication plan for devolution.

Third or cruising phase
As the start-up phase has not been completed and the ramp-up phase is still underway, the

cruising phase remains. It will consist in deepening the policy of deconcentration-devolution by building on the achievements and adapting to the realities of the field as a learning system.

One of the shortcomings of the current policy is the absence of a review of the decentralization policy from 2000 to date so that the results of this study can be used to refine the formulation of the new decentralization policy by drawing all the lessons from past experiences and taking into account the realities on the ground.

All of these projects are in progress and none is yet complete, which is the difficulty of implementing the devolution policy in Côte d'Ivoire, which we will analyze using a framework combining Bossert's decision space and Brinkerhoff's community empowerment.

6.2 In-depth analysis of devolution and coupling using the adapted framework combining Bossert's (1998) decision space and Brinkerhoff's (2006) community empowerment

Decentralization and devolution have been at the heart of health system reforms in low- and middle-income countries for decades. The aim is to bring services and decision-making closer to the users (1), to encourage community participation and to increase the responsiveness of health services to the needs of the population (3,16), as called for in the Alma Ata Declaration in 1978 (12).

Bossert developed an approach to estimate the degree of decentralization based on the transfer of decision making. The decision space tool proposes to examine the decision-making sphere in the four classifications of decentralization. As an instrument, it has been used to study the degree of choice made by decentralized structures in several developing countries (4,15-18).

Brinkerhoff discusses how bringing power closer to the people, or returning decision-making power to the people, could help expand democracy and strengthen the quality of health service delivery (3). He argues that decentralization can help improve community participation leading to population empowerment. The autonomous population can make its own choices about its national and local governments as well as about its health, education, agricultural and other needs (3).

In this study, we chose to use a framework adapted from Brinkerhoff (2006), which combines a modified Bossert (1998) decision space framework (4) with Brinkerhoff's (2006) community empowerment (3), to conduct an in-depth analysis of the current devolution-devolution coupling in Côte d'Ivoire. Bossert's framework was chosen for its applicability to low- and middle-income countries and because it explores how power over public choices is transferred from the central to the local government level. It is a pragmatic way to examine the complexity of choices and power relations between the center and the periphery (12,48).

> **Reviews**

However, a very salient criticism of this tool is that it is a formal map of the decision space that may not reflect the actual scope of decisions that the agent may have in countries where laws are not enforced or easily violated by the agent(12). The decision space is also important from the point of view of horizontal space, with respect to local actors. It will therefore be associated with Brinkerhoff's emphasis on community participation, capacity building leading to empowerment of local people to make the best choices for their own needs (3).

This community participation is specifically important in contexts with a weakened social fabric, such as in Côte d'Ivoire, where there is a need to rebuild social cohesion and trust between the central and local governments on the one hand and citizens or communities on the other (9,49).

We have therefore analyzed the deconcentration-devolution pairing in health in Côte d'Ivoire using this adapted framework. The decision space covers administrative, financial, fiscal, and political aspects (vertical decision space) and the degree of community empowerment (horizontal decision space), summarized in Table 5 below.

Table 5: Summary of the Decentralization-Devolution Pairing Using Decision Space and Community Empowerment

	On the administrative side	On the financial/fiscal level	On the political level	Degree of community empowerment
Discon-tration	• The creation, organization, attributions and functioning of the DRS and DDS are determined by the central level • Health policies, guidelines, standards and benchmarks are defined at the central level, and the DRS and DDS simply implement them according to central instructions • DRS and DDS personnel are recruited, assigned and distributed by the HRD from the central level (4)	• The DRS and DDS depend on the central level for their funding • MSHP and MEF determine the budget envelope and provide spending priorities • The DRS and DDS have no management autonomy but make expenditures according to budget lines defined by the central level without real control (4)	• All DRS and DDS agents and managers are civil servants recruited and appointed by the central level (MFP and MSHP), none are elected • They therefore serve the interests of the central level to which they are accountable (4)	• DRS and DDS have little interest in involving the population in health activities or in responding to local needs • There is a small space for the participation of local civil society to express the needs of the population, but the local elites control everything (3)
Devolution	• Health policies are defined at the central level, but their implementation on the ground is adapted to local priorities • The LGA sets local policies and priorities, planning autonomously in response to local needs and preferences but in harmony with national priorities. • The LGA builds and equips health facilities and makes them available to the MSHP. It also provides the health facilities with personnel that it pays. • The LGA receives civil servant personnel from the State but also recruits contractual personnel (4)	• LGs have fiscal and management autonomy • LGAs are not completely self-sufficient financially as the majority of their budget comes from the GC • The LGA has the ability to take out loans • The LGA takes stock of expenditures to local officials and citizens (4)	• The LGA is led by local elected officials • The LG has a strong local responsibility, he defines the budgetary priorities, the investments • The LG can develop decentralized cooperation and public-private partnership for the promotion of local development • The Ministry of the Interior exercises its supervision through an a posteriori control (4)	• The LGA has a strong interest in involving the population in health activities or responding to their needs • There is a great space for the participation of the local civil society to express the needs of the population • The degree of community empowerment increases with the participation of citizens in identifying and solving their own problems (3)

Framework adapted from Bossert 1998 and Brinkerhoff 2006 (3,4)

> Framework for analyzing the decentralization and devolution nexus using decision space and community empowerment

In Côte d'Ivoire, the Ministry of Health is composed of central and decentralized services. The deconcentrated services are represented by the Regional Health Departments (DRS), of which there are twenty, whose mission is to support the health districts in implementing the national health policy (36), and the Departmental Health Departments (DDS) or health districts, of which there are eighty-three, which are responsible for making the health policy operational (50).

The local governments (Collectivités Territoriales) are made up of thirty-one regions and one hundred and ninety-seven communes, with the task of providing for the needs of the population, promoting economic, social and cultural development and achieving national unity and cohesion, i.e. ensuring the overall development of their citizens (10).

The creation, organization, attributions and functioning of health regions and departments are determined by the Ministry of Health, while administrative regions and departments are created by the Ministry in charge of Territorial Administration or Ministry of the Interior. This situation leads to a mismatch between the health and administrative divisions, a source of leadership conflicts at the local level. Ideally, only the Ministry in charge of Territorial Administration should make the administrative division in which all other Ministries are involved.

Table 5 shows that each administration has its strengths and areas for improvement. In fact, the organization and functioning of the MSHP's deconcentrated services are determined by the central level, which determines their package of activities. They have no room for maneuver in their activities; they must comply with the policies, directives, standards, and guidelines defined at the central level, even if this does not fit with the realities in the field. The recruitment and assignment of health personnel as well as the equipment and maintenance of health facilities are done from the central level with the administrative slowness and heaviness that characterizes it. This could explain the inadequacies and poor distribution of human resources, as well as the dilapidated buildings and inadequate technical facilities observed at the local level (44). The room for maneuver of the DRSs and DDSs is limited in terms of innovation, individual initiatives, and adaptation of health action to local needs and population demand (4).

In addition, the deconcentrated services are run by civil servants recruited and appointed by the central level from which their operating budget comes. They have no independent source of income, no management autonomy and their expenditures are directed by pre-established budget lines without any real control. Corruption and a notorious lack of accountability are rife in this system, sometimes leading to embezzlement of public funds (51) and the conscious reduction of efforts through absenteeism (52). The sense of accountability of officials is therefore less oriented towards the population and more directed towards the central level, whose interests they serve in order to maintain their position or to obtain promotions in their work. They have little interest in involving the population in health activities or in responding to local needs. This leads to paternalistic attitudes that can go as far as demagoguery as described by Dugas and Dormael (53). These behaviors impede the delivery of essential services, undermine equity and development efforts (52), and do not promote community empowerment, which remains at a low level (3).

> **Strategic analysis**

These shortcomings can be ameliorated if deconcentrated services work in harmony with local governments that have more flexibility. Indeed, local government has the capacity to mobilize funds and the ability to adapt centrally defined policies to local priorities, to define policies and plan autonomously in response to local preferences and needs. In addition, the composition of regional and municipal councils is a mix of local elected officials from different political persuasions in proportion to election results (41). This makes it possible to form a local government that is representative of all local sensibilities for collaborative governance, thus helping to strengthen inter-community ties and reduce tensions in relations between the center and the periphery in a fragile country like Côte d'Ivoire (9,54).

Local elected officials are accountable to their constituents, to whom they report on actions taken and expenditures made, because it is the people who will be asked to reappoint them or sanction them at the next elections. Working in tandem with the deconcentrated services of the MSHP could contribute to improving the poor performance of governance indicators in health revealed by the General Health Inspectorate (51). Working together would also improve efficiency, rationality, and responsiveness in the management of local affairs due to the proximity of decision-making power, the speed of decision-making, and the permanent contact between citizens and leaders (2).

Deconcentration and devolution can improve community participation not in the utilitarian sense that it is initiated by health professionals who will convince individuals and the population to adhere to what they propose. Rather, it can be improved by a socio-political logic in which community participation is initiated and controlled by the community itself, enabling it to access quality information and resources (55,56). The community will thus be able to take action on its own to improve its own health and have greater control over its life (55,56). This participation, along with capacity building of local actors and a transfer of power and means, can consolidate the community and lead to progress towards community empowerment and more sustainable development (3).

 Critical analysis

However, deconcentration-devolution coupling is a highly complex co-existence process that will not be easy to implement because it involves human beings who may have divergent and contradictory expectations and interests. With the analysis of stake holders (Appendix 8 and 9), we will try to create coalitions and reduce tensions between actors in this dynamic, changing process in a fragile context. Moreover, in Côte d'Ivoire, democracy is not yet truly effective, and elections for local leaders are neither transparent nor open to all. Some local elected officials owe their positions not to the voters but to the leaders of the party in power, to whom they are accountable. They are therefore systematically re-elected at each election. As described in the literature review, these centrally supported local officials may be resistant to change and engage in embezzlement, corruption, patronage and clientelism for personal gain (57). As Brinkerhoff (2006) explained, some local elites want to monopolize decision-making and capture local resources. They therefore have less to gain from increased openness, transparency and direct citizen participation. They are then less likely to support community participation and empowerment efforts(3). Indeed, such participation is not possible without dialogue, nor without some degree of power sharing, for the more people are involved with correct, complete, and understandable information, the more power they gain, and conversely the power of leaders diminishes (55).

The possible adverse effects must be taken into account in the implementation of the devolution policy. Dealing with resistance from the local level requires political will and strong proactive intervention from the central level, for example, to expand the set of rights available to citizens and to put in place mechanisms to empower communities (3).

We therefore believe that if these two administrations, namely the deconcentrated services of the Ministry of Health and local governments, work together, putting at the service of the citizens the benefits that they could bring in terms of administration, finance, taxation, politics and community empowerment, the population would benefit. Thus, the participatory consensus-based health development planning process can serve as a precursor.

6.3 Analysis of the Planning Process

1.   Arguments in favor

We focus on the planning process because it is an ideal framework for implementing deconcentration-devolution coupling. Indeed, through planning, the different local stakeholders (local governments, deconcentrated services, communities, etc.) can together identify local problems and needs and solve them in a consensual manner. This process also brings the center closer to the periphery in the sense that the central actors become aware of the real local problems.

It can be a tool for harmonization and consensual coordination of activities at the local level. Participatory planning, accepted by all, mixed, especially bottom-up but also top-down; equitable planning that takes into account the diversity of opinion, minorities, gender, in which everyone is involved and which is implemented in a participatory and collegial manner, can help strengthen the coordination of activities at the level of local actors. In addition, the plan is an accountability tool, which gives credibility and reliability to the entity that has it. It allows for monitoring and evaluation of actions, improves the information and feedback cycle to adapt policies. It is also ideal for advocacy to mobilize resources at the national and international level. It is for all these reasons and more that we have chosen planning as one of the missions of my original department.

2.   Professional experience

The department in which I work in the Ministry of Health is the Department of Foresight, Planning, Evaluation and Health Information (DPPEIS), whose mission is, among other things, to contribute to making the deconcentration and devolution of the health sector operational (58). Thus, as part of these missions, we have carried out activities to help make the deconcentration-devolution policy effective in the health sector in Côte d'Ivoire, the main one being participatory regional planning for health development. From 2012 to 2014, out of the thirty-one administrative regions of the country, we initiated, with the technical support of Abt Associates Inc. and the financial support of PEPFAR/USAID, the development of Regional Health Development Plans (RHDP) in eight regions. Of the eight regions, which are Agnéby-Tiassa, Bélier, Guémon, Haut-Sassandra, Marahoué, Nawa, San Pedro and Sud-Comoé, the planning process has only been completed in four regions, namely Bélier, Guémon, Haut-Sassandra and Marahoué.

The development of the 2015-2017 PRDS was intended to be carried out in a participatory and inclusive framework with all health sector stakeholders at the regional level. The goal was to create a framework for collaboration and coordination of health action under the leadership of the Regional Council. The PRDS brought together actors from the Ministry of Health's decentralized services (ERS and ECD), actors from the regional and municipal councils, other technical ministries, users through civil society, NGOs, the private sector, and the technical and financial partner.

The process began with the development of training tools in planning methodology according to the Results-Based Management (RBM) model conducted by resource persons from the Ministry of Health and the Ministry of the Interior. Then, a pool of trainers and supervisors from the central level, twenty-two from the Ministries of Health and the Interior, were trained and equipped to replicate the training to local actors. At the level of each region, a training session on planning techniques was organized and attended by representatives of the local stakeholders listed above.

Two PRDS development workshops were organized with the facilitation of three resource persons from the central level and punctuated by working sessions between local actors. The PRDS is developed in several stages, including

- situational analysis,
- causal analysis,
- the results framework,
- the drafting of the plan document.

The architecture of the PRDS respects that of the current PNDS with the impact "the health status and well-being of the population are improved". The results framework is based on the six pillars of the WHO health system, which constitute its effects, namely

- Health sector leadership and governance are strengthened;
- health funding is improved;

- health human resources are improved;
- Quality health care benefits are improved;
- the availability and accessibility of medicines, vaccines and strategic inputs, infrastructure, materials and equipment (maintenance) are strengthened and
- the availability of quality health information is improved.

3. Critical analysis of the PRDS development process

The PRDS development process was conducted in a "top down" manner because local actors were not involved in the development of planning tools that should be adapted to the specificity of the local context. The training was theoretical and brief, and did not allow participants to master the participatory planning approach according to the RBM method, nor to correctly carry out the different steps of the plan development process. The implementation period of this strategic plan (PRDS 2015-2017) is short and not aligned with that of the PNDS 2016-2020.

In addition, USAID, through Abt Associates, practically imposed a planning approach that created tensions with resource persons at the central level. This dragged out the process, demotivated local actors, and caused the PRDS to fail in some regions. The national results framework did not always apply to local realities. Thus, the situational analysis should not be limited to the health indicators collected in the activity reports and reviews, but should also take into account the perceptions, expectations, and testimonies or difficulties experienced by the communities in the health facilities. All of this information should be translated into the form of problems for which solutions can be developed. However, some representatives of the facilities and populations were not the right people because they were designated by clientelism or by affinity with the leaders.

A plan cannot be written in two or three workshops, and no collaborative framework or small local committee for drafting the PRDS has been set up to finalize the drafting of the plan document outside the workshops. There has been no real transfer of skills to local actors for the sustainability of the PRDS development process. This could be explained by the lack of clarification of the roles and responsibilities of local governments (stewardship of the region), which should work in harmony with the deconcentrated services of the Ministry of Health. There was therefore no trust or commitment on the part of local actors, but rather a distrust of this top-down process in which community involvement was very low.

In addition, during this process, we were confronted with some difficulties due to the mismatch between the administrative and health territorial division. Indeed, the country has thirty-one administrative regions for twenty health regions, so one health region can cover two or three administrative regions. Sometimes, for the realization of a project, the Regional Director of Health faces the influence of three Presidents of regional councils who claim the lead and the implementation of the project on their territory. These tensions create difficulties that go beyond the regional framework and delay or even abort projects.

The PRDS should provide the region with a compass and an advocacy document for mobilizing resources and carrying out activities in a collegial manner within the framework of deconcentration-devolution coupling and make health action effective at the local level in order to achieve results. However, the inadequacy and inappropriateness of the texts and the absence of a decree implementing Law 2003-308 to specify the role and mandate of each, and therefore the absence of a real transfer of competencies and resources to local governments, has not allowed for the consensual and coordinated implementation of health activities. It is therefore important to propose strategies to remedy these problems.

7 Proposed Strategies

7.1 Vision

The vision of the deconcentration-devolution coupling in health is to strengthen the planning and coordination of health action at the local level in a horizontal governance (better collaboration) between the deconcentrated services of the MSHP with those of the local governments in order to bring closer and improve the offer of health services and care to all citizens, particularly the most vulnerable populations, and to sustain growth and local development.

This vision is supported by the values of equity, social justice, ethics, solidarity, rigor, transparency and accountability.

It is based on the principles of :

- Subsidiarity,

- vesting by operation of law,

- complementarity,

- no hierarchical or supervisory relationship between the Territorial Communities,

- the possibility of delegating the exercise of a power,

- need for prior consultation,

- democracy and community empowerment (11).

7.2 Strategic areas

We have developed four strategic axes to improve the implementation of the devolution coupling in Côte d'Ivoire. These are:

- strengthening the legislative, regulatory and institutional framework;

- capacity building of local actors;

- strengthening governance and accountability, and

- Improving local health development planning.

The strategic axes will be carried out with all stakeholders in an incremental, gradual process described by Lindblom (5) and a mixed top-down and bottom-up process described by Sabatier (6).

1- Strengthening the legislative, normative and institutional framework

The objective of this strategy is to remove any ambiguity and confusion by clarifying, through clear texts, the role and responsibility of each administration from local governments and ministerial deconcentrated services. It will contribute to the elaboration and revision of the remaining laws, notably the law on :

• the new configuration of the transfer and distribution of competences from the State to the Territorial Collectivities;

• the reform of the status of the personnel of the Local Authorities;

• the reform of the financial, fiscal and property regime of the Local Authorities.

It will then be able to propose all the application texts (decrees, ministerial or interministerial orders, etc.) relating to the transfer and distribution of health competences from the State to the Territorial Collectivities and to other laws.

Finally, this strategy will also be used to develop, revise and adapt the standards documents, procedures and benchmarks in the area of health (infrastructure, standard plans for health establishments, equipment, technical facilities, human resources, financial management, care and services, medicines, etc.) on which the local authorities will base their exercise of the health competencies that have been transferred to them.

This strategy will make it possible to update the law on the transfer of competencies and to issue the subsequent decrees. It will resolve the problems of legal vagueness, lack of transfer of means and clarification of local government responsibilities identified in the results. This will reduce mistrust between actors and promote community involvement in the design of PRDSs and the consensual implementation of activities.

2- Capacity building of local actors

The objective of this strategy is to empower all actors to appropriate and use the various texts (laws, decrees) relating to decentralization as well as health standards and benchmarks. With the participation of all stakeholders, it involves awareness-raising, dissemination, training and support sessions for local actors in the implementation (use) of skills. These steps in the knowledge transfer process described by the Institut National de Santé Publique de Québec (59) are shown in Figure 3 below.

Figure 3: Steps in the knowledge transfer process

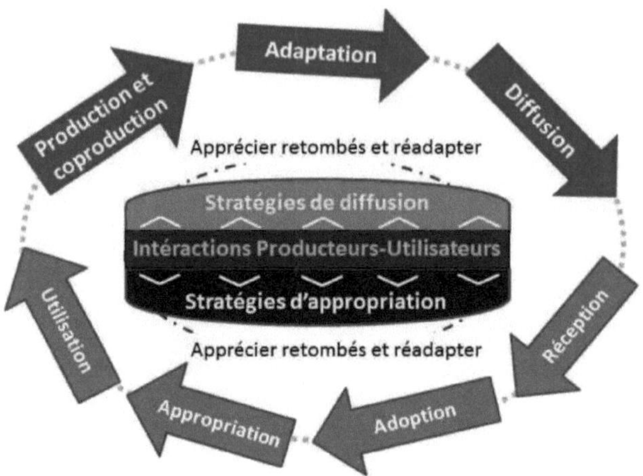

Source: Adapted from INSP Quebec, 2009 (59)

It will consist of a continuous, iterative, adaptive and learning process to strengthen the knowledge, skills and attitudes of local actors (human resources for health, local government personnel and communities). Through this strategy, the Direction de la Prospective, de la Planification, de l'Evaluation et de l'Information Sanitaire (DPPEIS), in collaboration with other stakeholders (DRS, DDS, MEMIS, LG, Civil Society, PTF, etc.), will organize training sessions and especially coaching for local actors to appropriate the participatory planning process and the content of laws, decrees and standards for construction, equipment and management of health facilities, etc. It will also contribute to solving the problem of the lack of a real transfer of knowledge and skills to local actors for the sustainability of the PRDS development process identified in the results. This process of transferring skills should not only be theoretical, but also and above all practical, through support in application and supervision. However, in order for the communities to truly evolve towards empowerment, this process of capacity building for local actors must be accompanied by a real transfer of powers (political, administrative, financial, fiscal, etc.), adequate means and take into account the specificity of the context (3).

3-   Strengthening governance and accountability

In this strategy, we will emphasize the culture of accountability and the strengthening of existing modes of governance at the local level. In addition to the existing vertical governance between the central level of the Ministry of Health and its deconcentrated services, the coupling of deconcentration and devolution will strengthen the collaboration and coordination relationships between actors at the same level (horizontal governance). Interactive governance must also be improved by better supervision of the interaction between state actors (LG, DRS, DDS, etc.) and non-state actors (technical and financial partners, NGOs, etc.) (30).

In fact, this strategy will make it possible to set up collaboration and coordination platforms between the various stakeholders, both at the central and local levels, with collaboration charters based on common interests and reciprocity (31). At the central level, these platforms will be set up between actors from the Ministry of Health, the Ministry of Territorial Administration, the umbrella organizations of the Territorial Collectivities (ADDCI and UVICOCI), the Territorial Collectivities themselves, civil society organizations and the TFPs. At the local level, platforms will be created between the deconcentrated services of the MSHP (DRS and DDS) and local governments (regions and communes), civil society, the community and the private health sector. As shown in Figure 4 below, while continuing to be accountable to the deconcentrated services, the accountability links of the health structures will be more pronounced in favor of the local governments.

Figure 4: Diagram of the hierarchical, functional and accountability links in the devolution coupling

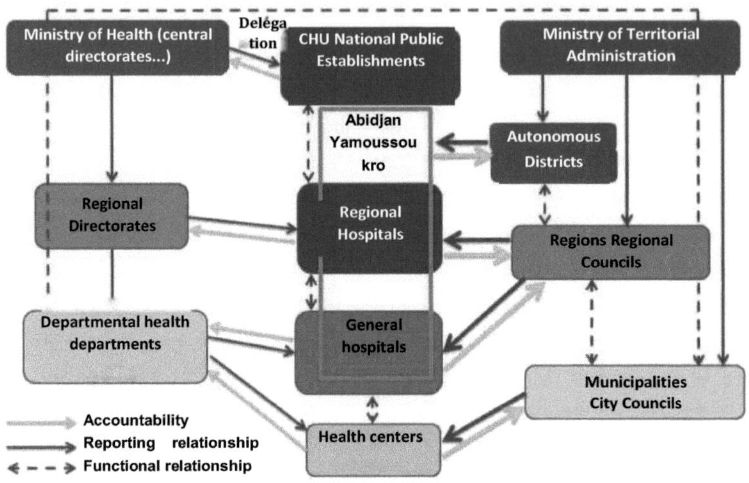

Source: Author, 2017

To improve accountability, transparency, and information sharing with the public, public accountability strategies (e.g., public review meetings, suggestion boxes) will be developed, as well as public involvement in the management committee of health facilities, in the local planning process, in setting local priorities, and in evaluating health action (31). To reduce corruption and misappropriation of public funds, graduated sanctions, including a written request for explanation, reprimand, suspension of pay, and dismissal, should be applied. To enhance extrinsic motivation, local actors who perform well will receive commendation diplomas and promotions with salary increases. To help stimulate intrinsic motivation, good practices will be shared within the municipality or region to serve as an example to other local governments. On the one hand, local actors have to adapt to the laws, regulations and standards produced by the central level, by changing their mentality and behavior. But on the other hand, the texts and norms must be readapted according to the realities on the ground (practical norms) (60,61).

4-   Improving the health development planning process

> Central planning

The process of developing the National Health Development Plan (NHDP) must be carried out within a broadly participatory and inclusive framework. It must bring together all the stakeholders in the health sector:

- central and peripheral public sector;
- the formal and informal private sector
- civil society (associations, NGOs, etc.);
- the population (clients or users)   ;
- development partners   ;
- etc.

The PNDS must take into account the new paradigms in health at the international level, but above all it must emphasize the national priorities in health. It must constitute the national compass from which other plans developed by both central and decentralized services, particularly the Regional Health Development Plans (PRDS), will derive.

> Planning at the local level

Our case study focuses on "coupling deconcentration and devolution through the regional health development planning process (RHDP), in the context of Côte d'Ivoire. The strategy for improving this process will allow the deconcentrated services of the Ministry of Health and local governments to work together with more credibility, in good collaboration and harmony. Governance and accountability can be improved through a participatory planning process involving all local stakeholders, implemented and evaluated together.

Indeed, the law gives each local authority the competence to develop and implement a health plan in harmony with the national plan. Our objective is to accompany local actors in the elaboration of a consensual PRDS, which is a strategic plan from which each party will draw its share to implement it in an annual action plan. The development of the PRDS will follow the architecture of the PNDS but with local priorities and needs. Three bodies will be essential to the development of the PRDS: the development committee, the steering committee and the technical committee for drafting the PRDS.

• **The drafting committee** will be composed of about twenty local actors from the decentralized services of the MSHP (DRS, DDS and 2 of their collaborators), the Territorial Collectivities (local elected officials and technicians in charge of social and health care and/or planning), the decentralized services of other Ministries (Prefectoral Corps, Education, Social Affairs, Economic Infrastructures, Plan and Development, Agriculture, etc.), civil society and other entities (private health care, NGOs, unions, orders, village and urban community leaders, associations, consumers, religious, local press, etc.).), civil society and other entities (private health care providers, NGOs, unions, orders, village and urban community leaders, associations, consumers, religious leaders, local press, etc.). This committee will have a role in designing the PRDS.

• **The steering committee** will be composed of the President of the Regional Council, who will chair it, and the Regional Director of Health, who will act as secretary. The members are the

Mayors of the region's municipalities; the President of the Regional Council's health commission and a representative of the private health sector. Its role will be to coordinate and supervise the PRDS development process; to ensure the effective drafting of the plan document within the specified timeframe and to ensure that the pre-established timetable is respected and that the results are achieved by the technical drafting committee.

• **The technical committee for the drafting of the PRDS** will be composed of the Regional Director of Health, who will be in charge of coordination, two technicians in charge of social health and/or planning within the Regional Council, the Head of the socio-cultural department of the regional capital city council and two health technicians. His role will be to :

- to provide technical assistance to the steering committee for all its activities;
- drafting the PRDS in accordance with the framework and timetable established under the supervision of the steering committee ;
- Present the PRDS at the validation and feedback workshops.

This small drafting committee, created at the local level to finalize the drafting of the plan document, will benefit from remote or face-to-face coaching from MSHP resource persons. The final plan document will then be submitted for validation to a larger body made up of the actors who participated in the drafting process and the heads of the local structures.

An Inter-ministerial Order signed by the Ministers of Territorial Administration and Health will formalize the three committees, giving them legitimacy and power to act. It will specify that the PRDS will be developed by the local governments (regions and communes) under the guidance of the Regional Council and the technical support of the decentralized services of the MSHP with the participation of all the stakeholders mentioned above. In particular, civil society, whose presence and consideration of its perceptions, expectations and testimonies will be mandatory in the PRDS development process.

To combat cronyism and the appointment of people by affinity with the leaders, the functions of the participants will be specified in the bylaw and a verification of the attendance lists with identification and professional documents will be carried out. A collaboration and work charter will be established to prevent problems and defuse tensions between the different stakeholders. Finally, advocacy will be done for the issuance of Inter-ministerial, Ministerial and Prefectural Orders to clarify the roles and responsibilities of the actors. This will help reduce mistrust, build confidence between actors and encourage community involvement in the development of the PRDS and its collegial implementation.

7.3 Implementation

Implementation will be done on a territory-wide scale, but through a process of gradual, incremental (5) transfer of competencies and means to local governments in the short, medium and long term.

> **In the short term**

Since the deconcentration-devolution tandem is written into the country's laws and strategy documents (PND and PNDS 2016-2020), it will be necessary to advocate for the creation of coalitions (62) within the Ministry of Health. It will be necessary to adopt a proactive approach to the management of stakeholders, exchanges, adaptation and consensus in order to :

- Set up an interdepartmental support unit for deconcentration and devolution (CIADD) in health;
- develop the devolution strategy paper in a bottom-up process;
- to propose the texts of laws, decrees, orders, directives, etc. to make the deconcentration-devolution couple functional, starting with the transfer of the competence of construction and equipment of health establishments to local governments. The transfer of the competence of management and maintenance of health establishments, a source of tension, will be postponed for the long term.
- strengthen the collaboration framework by setting up exchange platforms at all levels

> **In the medium term**

- to strengthen the capacities of the actors at the central and local levels;
- develop the regional health development plan (PRDS);
- implement competencies in a consensual manner, in a co-management of health establishments. The day-to-day management is the responsibility of the MSHP and the control through the presidency of the management committee is the responsibility of the local authority;
- Supervise, monitor, evaluate and readjust the different strategic axes. To draw lessons, both positive and negative, and to share experiences and good practices with other local authorities in a spirit of benchmarking.

> **Long term**

The long term will consist of monitoring and evaluating the short and medium term activities, the different strategic axes, and drawing lessons and building on the achievements in a cumulative process.
- transferring the management and maintenance of health facilities to the
local governments, after equipping them to carry it out.

- implement activities in a consensual manner, in a co-management of the
health facilities. All day-to-day management and chairing of the management committee is done by the local government. The MSHP providing a regulatory, supervisory and monitoring role for local health activities.

- supervise, monitor, evaluate and readjust by improving the previous phases and by evaluating the possibility of handing over more competences than initially planned.

8 Limitations

The process of decentralization being vast, complex, multidimensional, evolving, involving a diversity of stakeholders with changing positions, our work could not take into account all the factors. Since we cannot cover the entire process in this dissertation, we have chosen to focus on the impact of deconcentration-devolution on the local planning process.

The results of this work must therefore take into account several limitations. Because of time limitations, we were not able to interview political leaders and actors who played a key role in the various stages of the development and implementation of the decentralization policy. The work was very descriptive, as we needed more time for research and especially the exploitation of relevant publications and documents to deepen the analysis and enrich the discussion.

Similarly, the literature search could have gone beyond the databases described in the methodology to have more publications and arguments. We did not analyze other aspects of decentralization, such as delegation and privatization. The budgeting aspect of the planning process and the implementation of the PRDS was not addressed. The type and mode of governance in the deconcentration-devolution coupling has not been sufficiently developed and the analysis of the accountability of local elites is not thorough.

The study was conducted using published and unpublished secondary data, but mostly from our personal experience as we participated in most of the processes described in this dissertation. Hence, the importance of the descriptive part of the study which constitutes a wealth of information for the reader but it can also constitute a source of bias.

9 Recommendations

The following recommendations are necessary to improve and contribute to the successful implementation of the devolution policy in health in Côte d'Ivoire. They are based on the results of our study.

1. To national actors

- **Presidency of the Republic**

J Translate the political **will** into a strong and sincere political **commitment** to boost the adoption of the remaining texts and align all the actors with the measures decided in a consensual manner for a real implementation of the decentralization policy in Côte d'Ivoire

J Make the decision-making process less top-down and more participatory, by involving the various stakeholders through their representatives.

Government

Make concessions, compromise and support the decentralization process by effectively ceding powers and competencies to the Territorial Collectivities.

J Make available to the Territorial Communities the resources (human, financial, material and time) adequate for the exercise of the transferred competencies. This is to enable local actors to better support the central level in carrying out its missions

- **Ministry of State, Ministry of Interior and Security (MEMIS)**

J To carry out, with all stakeholders, the assessment of the decentralization policy from 2000 to the present so that the results of this study can be used to refine the formulation of the new decentralization policy by drawing all the lessons from past experiences and taking into account the realities on the ground ;

J Take into account the perceptions and interests of all current central and local actors in order to redefine the policy of decentralization and the transfer and distribution of competencies from the State to the Territorial Collectivities;

J Readapting the "law n°2003-308 of July 7, 2003 on the transfer and distribution of competences from the State to the Territorial Collectivities" (11) by maintaining communal competences and regrouping all supra communal competences at the level of the Region;

J To be part of an incremental process of gradual transfer of competences and means from the State to local governments in order to make it acceptable to other ministries;

J Develop a more active and committed communication strategy to raise awareness and disseminate the texts on decentralization and the transfer of competencies to all stakeholders;

J Facilitate and take an active part, as guardian of the Territorial Collectivities, in the actions carried out by the other Ministries in the framework of decentralization.

- **Ministry of Health and Public Hygiene (MSHP)**

J Develop a strategy document for the implementation of the deconcentration-devolution policy in the health sector that could serve as a compass for the Ministry of Administration to update the law on the transfer and distribution of competencies from the State to the Territorial Communities;

J As soon as possible, issue the implementing decrees for the laws in order to specify the implementation procedures with the roles and responsibilities of each stakeholder;

In collaboration with the Ministry of Administration, establish an Inter-ministerial Support Unit for Deconcentration-Devolution (CIADD) in health. In addition to its capacity building and support role, the CIADD will have more binding powers and responsibilities for the parties involved. If successful, it could be gradually extended to other sectors;

J **Establish** platforms for collaboration and exchange at both the central and local levels to facilitate the coordination and implementation of the devolution strategy;

J Adapt the regional health division to the regional administrative division so that the Regional Director of Health has a single point of contact to facilitate collaboration between the regional health team and the Regional Council;

Strengthen support for the process of developing Regional Health Development Plans (RHDPs) and their implementation under the leadership of the Regional Council. This will reduce the fragmentation of health action and strengthen coordination and governance;

Revise, in a bottom-up and dynamic process, the guidelines and standards documents to adapt them to the new decentralization architecture. This will facilitate ownership and implementation by all actors;

J To monitor and evaluate the exercise of transferred health competencies.

- **Professional associations and health workers**

Support the process initiated by the Ministry of Health by sharing your experiences at all stages; because the commitment of the actors in the field is a determining factor in the success of all initiatives.

- **Local authorities**

J Adhere to the incremental process of gradual transfer of competences and means from the State to the Territorial Collectivities for a progressive appropriation of competences;

J Support and engage in collaborative and capacity-building actions initiated by the Ministry of Health and the Ministry of Administration;

Own and sustain the participatory planning process with all local stakeholders. Consensus-based implementation of PRDSs can improve governance and coordination of local health action;

Mobilize local resources, improve accountability and ensure transparency in the management of public resources. This requires a change in behavior and a real involvement of the population in the identification of priorities and the execution of expenditures.

- **Researchers and academics**

Conduct and publish more research on the process of adoption and implementation of decentralization policy in general and in the health sector in Côte d'Ivoire. It is important to have the results of studies conducted locally to enrich the analyses. This work will provide valuable information on the weaknesses of the process and best practices that can guide the adaptation of implementation through the design of strategies adapted to the specificities of the country.

2. To international players

Provide adequate technical and financial assistance to national actors for the implementation of the decentralization process in Côte d' Ivoire. This includes aligning donor funding with the country's priorities, monitoring, evaluation and accountability.

10 Conclusion

Our study analyzed the decentralization policy in the health sector in Côte d'Ivoire, focusing on the operationalization of the deconcentration and devolution couple through the local participatory planning process. Indeed, decentralization is a topical issue that affects all sectors of activity in many low- and middle-income countries, including Côte d'Ivoire. Its legitimacy is based on the grounds of efficiency, rationality, responsiveness of services to the needs of the population and its capacity to increase community participation. Also, despite resistance, the Ministry of Health has undertaken actions to make decentralization functional, particularly in the form of deconcentration and devolution in the health sector. In our study, which is in line with this vision, we propose four main strategic axes to make the deconcentration and devolution couple operational. This is a complex, iterative process that must be implemented in an incremental, gradual and participatory manner, taking into account the interests of the various stakeholders. This operationalization requires intelligent collaboration between the decentralized services of the Ministry of Health and local governments through a broadly participatory, mixed top-down and bottom-up planning process and consensual coordination of health activities at the local level.

Bibliography

1.   Brinkerhoff, Derick W; Johnson RW. Good Enough Governance in Fragile States: the Role of Center-Periphery Relations and Local Government. Ankara, Turkey; 2008. (Workshop No. 3: Making the good enough governance agenda realistic).

2.   Koffi A, Tere G, Mel T. Decentralization and economic crisis in Côte d'Ivoire: The case of General Council of Dimbokro. Eur Sci Journal, ESJ. 2013;9(25):85-109.

3.   Brinkerhoff DW, Azfar O. Decentralization and community empowerment: does community empowerment deepen democracy and improve service delivery? US Agency Int Dev. 2006;(October):1-43.

4.   Bossert T. Analysing the decentralisation of health systems in developing countries: decision space, innovation and performance. Soc Sci Med. 1998;47(10): 147-60.

5.   Lindblom CE. The Science of "Muddling Through." Public Adm Rev. 1959;19(2):79-88.

6.   Sabatier PA. Top-Down and Bottom-Up Approaches to Implementation Research: a Critical Analysis and Suggested Synthesis. J Public Policy. 1986;6(1):21.

7.   Rondinelli DA, Nellis JR, Shabbir Cheema G. Decentralization in Developing Countries A Review of Recent Experience [Internet]. 1983 (World Bank staff). Available from: http://documents.worldbank.org/curated/en/868391468740679709/pdf/multi0page.pdf

8.   Pariente A. The state, decentralization and the economic crisis: reconciling the irreconcilable?
[Internet]. 2012 [cited2017Jun11]. Availablefrom: http://www.metropolitiques.eu/IMG/pdf/MET-Pariente.pdf

9.   Brinkerhoff DW, Johnson RW. Decentralization of local governance in the Fragile states: lessons from the Iraqi case. Rev Int des Sci Adm.

2009;75(4):643.

10.   Ministry in charge of territorial administration. Law No. 2014-451 of 05 August 2014 on the orientation of the general organization of the Territorial Administration [Internet]. DGDDL. Abidjan, RCI; 2014 [cited 2017 Jun 14]. p. 9. Available from: http://www.dgddl.interieur.gouv.ci/?page=cadre&cat=loi

11.   Ministry in charge of territorial administration. Law n°2003-208 of July 7, 2003 on the transfer

and distribution of competences from the State to the territorial authorities [Internet]. DGDDL. 2003 [cited 2017 Jun 14]. Available from: http://www.dgddl.interieur.gouv.ci/?page=cadre&cat=loi

12.   Mohammed J, North N, Ashton T. Decentralization of Health Services in Fiji: A Decision Space Analysis. Int J Heal Policy Manag. 2016 Nov 15;5(3):173-81.

13.   Lucy Gilson, Peter Kilima MT. Local government decentralization and the health sector in Tanzania. Public Adm Dev. 1994;14(5):451-477.

14.   Jennie Litvack, Junaid Ahmad RB. Rethinking Decentralization in Developing Countries. World Bank Econ Sect Work Decentralization. 1998;

15.   Berman PA, Bossert TJ. A Decade of Health Sector Reform in Developing Countries: What Have We Learned? In: DDM Symposium on Appraising a Decade of Health Sector Reform in Developing Countries. 2000. p. 0-20.

16.   Bossert T, Chitah MB, Bowser D. Decentralization in Zambia: resource allocation and district performance. Health Policy Plan. 2003 Dec;18(4):357-69.

17.   Bossert TJ, Larranaga O, Giedion U, Arbelaez JJ, Bowser DM. Decentralization and equity of resource allocation: evidence from Colombia and Chile. Bull World Health Organ. 2003;81(2):95-100.

18.   Bossert, Thomas; Beauvais J. Decentralization of health systems in Ghana, Zambia, Uganda and the Philippines: a comparative analysis of decision space. Health Policy Plan. 2002 Mar;17(1):14-31.

19.   Brinkerhoff DW, Wetterberg A, Wibbels E. Distance, services, and citizen perceptions of the state in rural Africa. Governance. 2017;(May 2016):1-22.

20.   MARIE J, IDELMAN E. THE decentralization in West Africa: a revolution in local governance? EchoGeo. 2012;13(2010):14.

21.   Brinkerhoff D. Introduction - Governance Challenges in Fragile States: Reestablishing Security, Rebuilding Effectiveness, and Reconstituting Legitimacy. DW Brinkerhoff Gov Post-Conflict Soc Rebuilding Fragile States. 2007;23.

22.   Bado J-P. Colonial medicine and major endemics in Africa 1900-1960: leprosy, human trypanosomiasis and onchocerciasis. Collections Hommes et sociales. Éditions Karthala; 1996. 432 p.

23.   WHO & UNICEF. Report of the international conference on primary health care [Internet]. Alma-Ata   (USSR);   1978   [cited   2017   Jun   13].   p.   90.   Available   from: http://apps.who.int/iris/bitstream/10665/39243/1/9242800001.pdf

24.   Ministry of Health. Order No. 741 defining the minimum activity package. RCI; 1996. p. 11.

25.   Ministry of Health of Côte d'Ivoire. National health policy document. RCI; 2012. p. 37.

26.   Mills A, Vaughan JP, Smith DL, Tabibzadeh I. Decentralization of health systems: concepts, problems, and experiences of selected countries. World Heal Organ. 1991;174.

27.   Gilson L. Health policy and systems research: methodology manual: abridged version. 2012;112.

28.   Leichter H. A Comparative Approach to Policy Analysis: Health Care Policy in Four Nations. Cambridge Univ Press. 1979;

29.   Johnson G, Scholes K. Fundamentals of strategy. Management. Financial Times Prentice Hall; 2002. 313 p.

30.   Van Belle S, Mayhew SH. Public accountability needs to be enforced -a case study of the governance arrangements and accountability practices in a rural health district in Ghana. BMC Health Serv Res. 2016;16(1):568.

31.   Van Belle S, Mayhew SH. Public accountability practices of district health management teams: a realist inquiry in two local health systems in Ghana. BMC Health Serv Res. 2014;14:P134.

32.   Bell S Hindmoor A. Rethinking Governance: The Centrality of the State in Modern Society. Aust J Public Adm. 2009;

33.   Sorensen, E. Torfing J. "Making governance networks effective and democratic through metagovernance." Public Adm. 2009;87(2):234-258.

34.   Walt G, Shiffman J, Schneider H, Murray SF, Brugha R, Gilson L. "Doing" health policy analysis: Methodological and conceptual reflections and challenges. In: Health Policy and Planning. 2008. p. 308-17.

35.   Ministry of Planning and Development. Recensement Général de la Population et de l'Habitat RGPH 2014. National Institute of Statistics. Abidjan, RCI; 2014.

36.   Ministry of Health. Order No. 007/MSLS/CAB of February 02, 2012 appointing the Regional Directors of Health and AIDS Control. 2012. p. 10.

37.   Ministry of Health / Ministry of Planning. Demographic and Health Survey with Multiple Indicators (EDS-MICS). Abidjan, RCI; 2012.

38.   World Bank. Côte d'Ivoire [Internet]. 2015 [cited 2017 Jun 16]. Available from: http://www.banquemondiale.org/fr/country/cotedivoire

39. UNDP. Human Development Report 2014. Sustaining human progress: reducing vulnerabilities and building resilience. 2014. 259 p.

40. Ministry in charge of territorial administration. Law n°2001-476 of August 9, 2001 Orientation on general organization of territorial administration [Internet]. DGDDL. Abidjan, RCI; 2001 [cited 2017 Jun 14]. Available from: http://www.dgddl.interieur.gouv.ci/?page=cadre&cat=loi

41. Ministry in charge of territorial administration. Law n°2012-1128 of December 13, 2012 on the organization of territorial authorities [Internet]. DGDDL. 2012 [cited 2017Jun14   ]. p.   46. Availablefrom   : http://www.dgddl.interieur.gouv.ci/?page=cadre&cat=loi

42. Ministry of Health. National Health Development Plan 2009-2013. Abidjan, RCI: MSHP; 2009. p. 174.

43. Ministry of Planning and Development. Household living standards survey (ENV 2015). Abidjan, RCI; 2015.

44. Ministry of Health. National health development plan 2016-2020. Abidjan, RCI; 2016.

45. Alasane Ouattara. Summary of the "Living Together" program [Internet]. 2010 [cited 2017 Jun14]. Available from: http://www.ado.ci/images/programme_complet_de_ado.pdf

46. Ministry in charge of territorial administration. Decree No. 2012-612 of July 04, 2012 establishing the Moronou Region [Internet]. DGDDL. 2012 [cited 2017 Jun 21]. Available from: http://www.dgddl.interieur.gouv.ci/?page=cadre&cat=loi

47. Ministry in charge of territorial administration. Decree No. 2011-263 of September 28, 2011 on the organization of the national territory into Districts and Regions [Internet]. DGDDL. 2011 [cited 2017 Jun 21]. Available from: http://www.dgddl.interieur.gouv.ci/?page=cadre&cat=loi

48. Faguet J-P. Low Decision Space Means No Decentralization in Fiji Comment on " Decentralization of Health Services in Fiji: A Decision Space Analysis " Commentary. Kerman Univ Med Sci. 2016;5(511):663-665.

49. Soura BD, Coulibaly SS. [Analysis of the healthcare service decentralization process in Côte d'Ivoire]. Med Sante Trop. 24(2):151-6.

50. Ministry of Health. Order No. 0121/MSLS/CAB of May 03, 2012 appointing Departmental Directors of Health and AIDS Control. 2012. p. 4.

51. Ministry of Health. Evaluation of Health Sector Governance in Cote d'Ivoire. 2014;

52.   World Bank, International Finance Corporation. World Development Report: Governance and the law. 2017.

53.   Dugas S, Dormael M Van. The construction of family medicine in developing countries. Vol. 22, Studies in Health Services Organisation & Policy. 2003.

54.   Barron, P and Clark S. Decentralizing Inequality? Center-Periphery Relations , Local Governance , and Conflict in Aceh. Soc Dev Pap. 2006;(39).

55.   Rifkin SB, Muller F, Bichmann W. Primary health care: on measuring participation. Soc Sci Med. 1988;26(9):931-40.

56.   Bichmann W, Rifkin SB, Shrestha M. Can we measure the degree of participation community? Forum Mond Sante. 1989;10:513-8.

57.   Brinkerhoff DW, Goldsmith AA. Clientelism, Patrimonialism and Democratic Governance: an overview and framework for Assessment and Programming. ... , MD

Abt Assoc 2002) http//pdf.... 2002;(January 2015):49.

58.   Ministry of Health. Decree No. 2016-598 of 03 August 2016 on the organization of the Ministry of Health and Public Hygiene. 2016;

59.   Lemire, Nicole; Souffez, Karine; Laurendeau M-C. Facilitating a knowledge transfer process. Bibliothèque et archives nationales du Québec. Quebec City; 2009.

60.   Olivier De Sardan J-P. The eight modes of local governance in West Africa. Working paper. 2009.

61.   Olivier de Sardan J-P. Les gouvernances locales, la délivrance des biens publics, et les redevabilités. In: Decentralization: legitimacy and governance A process of recomposition of local powers. 2011. p. 1-9.

62.   Sabatier PA. An advocacy coalition framework of policy change and the role of policy-oriented learning therein. Policy Sci. 1988;21(2-3):129-68.

Annexes

Appendix 1: Description of the research strategy used

The search of the English and French literature was conducted using the search engines Medline (pubmed), Google Scholar and the online databases of the Institute of Tropical Medicine (ITM) and other regional research institutes (CODESRIA, LASDEL, etc.) with key words (policy, decentralization, devolution, transfer of competencies, health)

In **Google Scholar** and online library databases, the keywords we used to search were Decentralization health

In **Medline (PubMed) whenever possible, the** MeSH terms that were used were "Decentralization", "health", "policy", "devolution", "Decentralization health", "policy health", "Transfer skills"

From this combination: **(((((Health) AND Policy)) AND Decentralization)) AND ((Devolution) OR ((transfer) AND skills))**

Search details: (("health" [MeSH Terms] OR "health" [All Fields]) AND ("policy" [MeSH Terms] OR "policy" [All Fields]) AND ("politics" [MeSH Terms] OR "politics" [All Fields] OR "decentralization" [All Fields]) AND (Devolution [All Fields] OR ("transfer (psychology)" [MeSH Terms] AND "(psychology)" [All Fields]) OR "transfer (psychology)"[All Fields] OR "transfer"[All Fields]) AND skills[All Fields])

We obtained 59 results in MEDLINE (PUBMED).

We also obtained 487 initial results in Google Scholar

Appendix 2: Raw search results from Medline and Google Scholar

Search	Add to builder	Query	Items found	Time
#13	Add	Search (((((Health) AND Policy)) AND Decentralization)) AND ((Devolution) OR ((transfer) AND skills))	59	10:04:29
#12	Add	Search (Devolution) OR ((transfer) AND skills)	3729	10:04:09
#11	Add	Search (((Health) AND Policy)) AND Decentralization	15202	10:03:22
#10	Add	Search (((Health) AND Policy)) AND ((Decentralization) OR ((transfer) AND skills))	15274	10:02:01
#9	Add	Search (Decentralization) OR ((transfer) AND skills)	58482	10:01:43
#8	Add	Search (Health) AND Policy	250023	10:00:25
#7	Add	Search (transfer) AND skills	3298	09:58:22
#6	Add	Search skills	152474	09:57:55
#5	Add	Search transfer	429720	09:56:37
#4	Add	Search Devolution	431	09:56:24
#3	Add	Search Decentralization	55191	09:56:12
#2	Add	Search Health	3742333	09:55:59
#1	Add	Search Policy	323890	09:55:47

Google

Scholar

allintitle: Decentralization health

Environ 487 résultats (0,06 s)

Mes citations

Articles

Ma bibliothèque

Date indifférente
Depuis 2017
Depuis 2016
Depuis 2013
Période spécifique...

1990 — 2017

Rechercher

Trier par pertinence
Trier par date

Toutes les langues
Rechercher les pages en Français

inclure les brevets
inclure les

Conseil : Recherchez des résultats uniquement en **Français**. Vous pouvez indiquer votre langue de recherche sur la page Paramètres Google Scholar.

Decentralization, health care and policy process in the Punjab, Pakistan in the 1990s
CD Collins, M Omar, E Tarin - ... International journal of health ..., 2002 - Wiley Online Library
Abstract The Province of the Punjab underwent a number of attempts to decentralize the **health** sector in the 1990s. Among the most important were the **decentralization** of financial management within the district, the Sheikhupura PHC Pilot Project, the establishment of the
Cité 82 fois   Autres articles   Les 9 versions   Citer   Enregistrer   Plus
[PDF] researchgate.net

[LIVRE] Federalism and **decentralization** in European **health** and social care
J Costa-Font, S Greer - 2016 - books.google.com
This is the first book to examine the processes of territorial federalization and **decentralization** of **health** systems in Europe drawing from an interdisciplinary economics, public policy and political science approach. It contains key theoretical and empirical
Cité 25 fois   Autres articles   Les 5 versions   Citer   Enregistrer   Plus

Analyzing the **decentralization** of **health** systems in developing countries: decision space, innovation and performance
T Bossert - Social science & medicine, 1998 - Elsevier
Decentralization has long been advocated as a desirable process for improving **health** systems. Nevertheless, we still lack a sufficient analytical framework for systematically studying how **decentralization** can achieve this objective. We do not have adequate means
Cité 479 fois   Autres articles   Les 33 versions   Citer   Enregistrer   Plus
[PDF] sti.ch

Decentralization of **health** systems in Ghana, Zambia, Uganda and the Philippines: a comparative analysis of decision space
TJ Bossert, JC Beauvais - Health policy and planning, 2002 - Oxford Univ Press
Abstract This study reviews the experience of **decentralization** in four developing countries:
[PDF] oxfordjournals.org

Overview of the research process

(20/05/2017 - 20/06/2017)

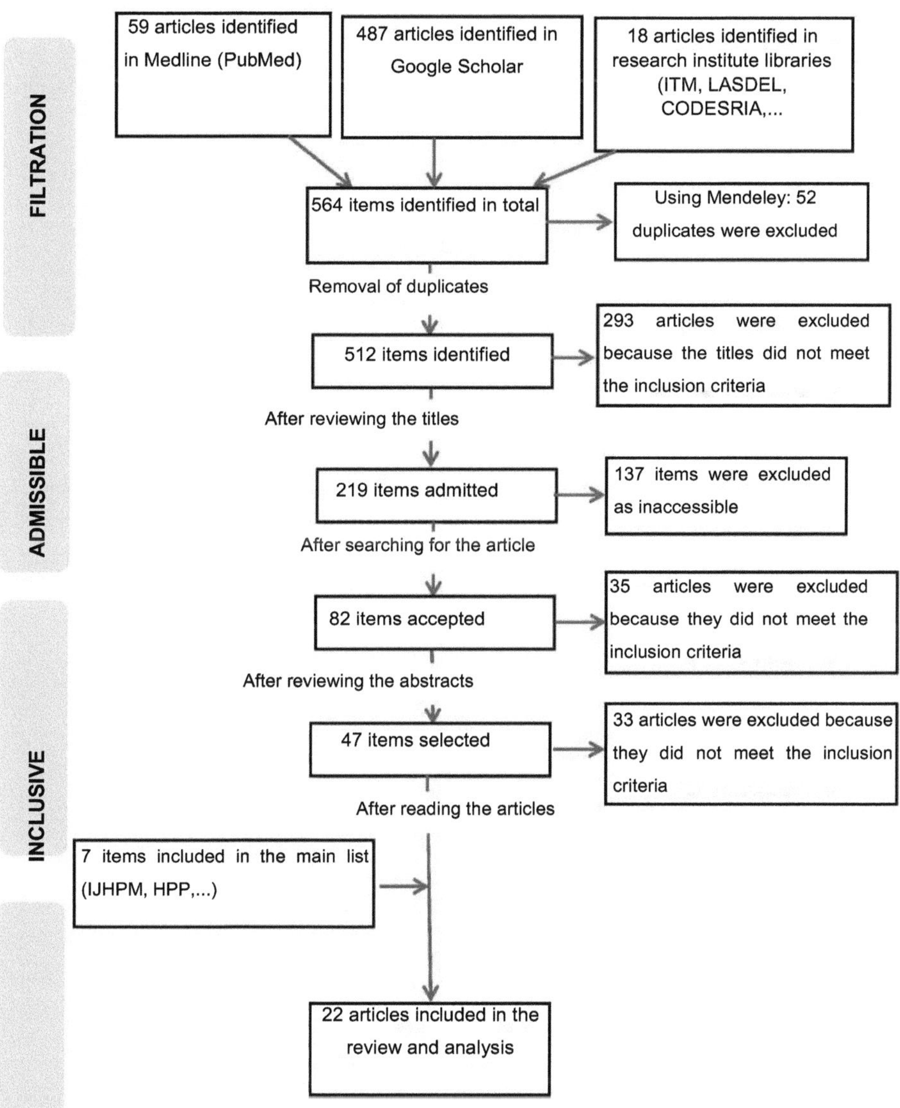

Appendix 4: Maps of the health and administrative regions of Côte d'Ivoire

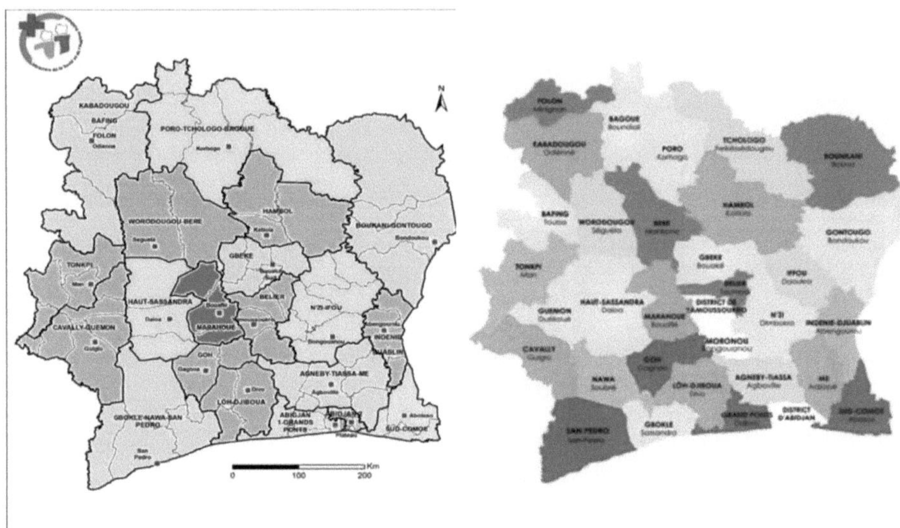

20 Health regions

Source: MSHP/DPPEIS/RASS 2015

31 Administrative regions

Source: adapted from http://a403.idata.over-blog.com/
450x500/1/40/60/97/cote-d-ivoire/carte-Cote-d-ivoire.jpg

Appendix 5: Distribution of Côte d'Ivoire among the belligerents

Source : https://espacepolitique.revues.org/docannexe/image/894/img- 4-small580.jpg 2003

Annex 6: Summary of the sixteen areas of competence transferred from the State to local governments

THE TRANSFERRED COMPETENCES COVER THE FOLLOWING SIXTEEN (16) AREAS:	
1 °) land use planning	9°) education, scientific research and professional and technical training
2°) the planning of the development	10°) social, cultural and human promotion action
3°) urban planning and housing	11 °) sports and leisure
4°) communication routes and various networks	12°) the promotion of economic development and employment
5°) transport	13°) promotion of tourism
6°) health, public hygiene and quality	14°) communication
7°) the protection of the environment and natural resource management	15°) water, sanitation and electrification
8°) security and civil protection	16°) the promotion of the family, youth, women, children, the handicapped and people of 3®"* age

Source: Law n°2003-208 of July 7, 2003(11)

Appendix 7: Distribution of health responsibilities transferred to local governments

1) Development and implementation of local health, public hygiene and quality control plans in harmony with the national plan	
2) Issuance of opinions on the prospective development of the national health map	
3) Adoption of preventive measures in the field of health, public and food hygiene	
4) Construction, Management and Maintenance:	
Local governments	**Health structures**
Regional Council	Regional hospitals
General Council	General hospitals
District Council	General hospitals and public health and food establishments
City Council	General hospitals and public health and food establishments
City Council	Health centers or First Contact Health Establishments (FCHE)

Source: Law No. 2003-208 of 7 July 2003(11)

Annex 8: Key stakeholders involved in the devolution process and strategies for policy dialogue with them

Actors directly involved	Actors indirectly involved
Presidency Republic Parliament Government Ministry of Health: Cabinet, DPPEIS, DGS, DRS, DDS Health professionals .... Ministry of Administration (Interior) Regions: the President of the Regional Council and his office Municipalities: the Mayor and the Municipal Council Local government umbrella organizations: the presidents of ARDCI and UVICOCI and their boards	Population Representatives of international agencies (WHO, World Bank, EU, UNDP,...) Universities of Côte d'Ivoire National NGOs Colleges, unions and professional associations Formal and informal private health sector Mass media Ministry of Economy and Finance, Ministry of Planning and Development

Source: Author, 2017

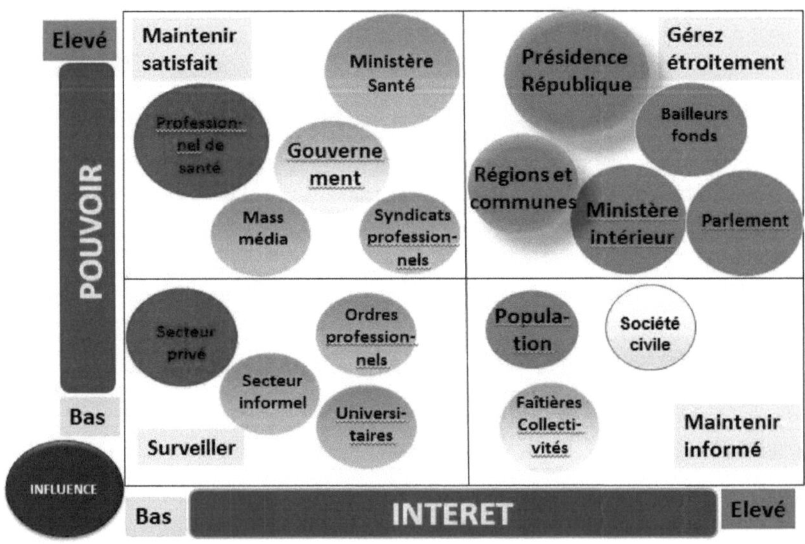

Source: adapted from G. Johnson & K. Scholes, 2002.

STAKE HOLDERS	ROLE / INVOLVEMENT	INTERESTS	INFLUENCE / POWER	RESOURCES	POSITION	IMPACT
Health professionals (DDS, DRS)	Opposes the policy	Low: Consciousness change senseredevability loss of earnings	Bottom: Provide care Resist	Strikes practical standards £ official standards	Counter Passive observer	Limit and slow down implementation
Colleges, unions and professional associations	Opposes political aspects threaten members	Bottom: defends the interests of its members for survival	Bottom: watch medical deontology counteract	Edit Codes Government Strikes	Ambiguous Interpell Passive observer	Limit and defer pending effects
Beneficiaries Population	Benefits	Top: hopes to improve access to quality care and well-being	Social mobilization force government	Manisfesta-tion to support/ reject to vote	Adheres Passive Right observer	Limit and defer pending effects
Regions and municipalities	Implements Benefits	Top: increases power to have positive image Re-election	Top: Working success reform	Mobilization of local and external resources	Supports the policy and accompanies	Top : Accelerates implementation
Presidency Republic	Policy Initiator / Advocate	Top: Election Promise Re-election	Top: Resignation, sanction, revocation	State budget State resources commitment	For and to make political promotion	Top: Accelerate implementation
Government (Health, Interior,…)	Develops sector content (health) and implements	Medium: Mixed Fear of disappointing president Retain authority/ skills	Means: Mitigate content reduce skills to be transferred	National expertise Administrative burden Do not propose decree	Mitigated and promote political watering down conformism	Top: Slowed implementation Lack of proposal for decrees
Parliament	Amends and adopts decentralized texts	Means: Take texts for the good of their constituents	Medium: Legislative power but follows decisions President	Legislate Possibility to modify the texts	For the policy	Top: Accelerate implementation
Local government umbrella organizations (ARDCP, UVICOCI*)	Coordinates implementation Benefits	Top: defends elected interests survival Reconducted	Bottom: Watching over the region and the community	Solidarity between territorial communities	Political support and promotion	Means: Facilitate implementation
Civil society (academics, political activists, associations, NGOs, media)	Alerters Watching over the interests of the people	Medium: member population hopes for a better life	Means: To generate social mobilization	Mobilization Slots Scientific Articles Meeting	For and to facilitate the implementation	Medium: Accelerates implementation
Formal and informal private sector	Opposes the policy	Bottom: Reduce customer base not pay more taxes	Bottom: Provide care	Networks of health structures Patient attraction	Against the reform	Limit but slow down policy implementation
Donors International agencies	Accompany. Watch	Medium: hopes advanced to eus	Bottom: Pressure, technicality	Financial and technical support Diplomacy	Adheres to and facilitates the implementation	Medium: Accelerates implementation

*UVICOCI: Union Villes et Communes de Côte d'ivoire

For all comments and suggestions, please leave a message at

alloukouar@gmail.com

Printed by Books on Demand GmbH, Norderstedt / Germany